I may be old but I've

ALL THE COOL BANDS

One fan's story about why music matters!

KEN SCHWARTZ

I May Be Old but I've Seen All the Cool Bands: One Fan's Story about Why Music Matters!

Visit our website at **www.StillwaterPress.com** for more information.

First Stillwater River Publications Edition

ISBN: 978-1-955123-23-5

1 2 3 4 5 6 7 8 9 10
Written by Ken Schwartz
Cover design by Craig Bower
Book design by Craig Bower & Emma St. Jean
Published by Stillwater River Publications, Pawtucket, RI, USA.

For: Mum, Val, Tim, Ian, Ben, Dog, and Kit.

And for new grandson, Kaiden.
Can't wait to take you to your first show!

Con

tents

Acknow

To Greg Renoff, author of two ridiculously awesome Rock n Roll books, Ted Templeman: A Platinum Producer's Life in Music (by Ted Templeton, as told to Greg Renoff) and Van Halen Rising: How a Southern California Backyard Party Band Saved Heavy Metal, which every 70s-80s rock fan needs to read, like right now. I appreciate your advice and most importantly, pushing me to get off my ass to write this book.

To Def Leppard—you guys are the band I've loved the longest and the one that got me into really good Rock n Roll. I just wanted to say thanks in the hopes that one day you can come say you're welcome—the bar tab is on me.

ledgements

To Craig Bower, my designer, and my metal brother, just simply thank you. You rock, your designs rock, and your KISS man cave is something everyone should stop by and see if you're in Green Bay, WI. And to his awesome family, Jen, Carly, and Ellie, for letting me pull him away from you as he helped design this book. He's a talented artist and I highly encourage every single one of you who reads this to work with him too at www.designthatrocks.com.

To Val, Tim, Ian, Ben, and Kaiden–I do this all for you so 30 years from now, you can look back and say 'wow Dad, you really were a complete and utter Rock n Roll dork,' which I'm sure you already do.

To Mum and Jack–just for being there, and for letting me finally call you out as the Hippie you are, mum. Love ya.

To my wife, Kitty. When we first met, you didn't know the Doors from Zeppelin, which just blew me away. But 7+ years, and dozens of concerts later (including waaaaay too many with Styx and REO Speedwagon), you blow me away with how much music you DO know, and just how amazing you are. You are my Rock n Roll partner, my musical muse, and the one I simply can't live without. I guess I'll keep on loving you....

And finally, to all the rock stars out there, either the ones on the stage or the ones in the audience. This is for you. Keep sharing your Rock n Roll experiences. Keep the rock alive. Keep the music coming. Keep writing great books. And always, rock the fuck on! \m/

For

eword

When you have been doing Rock n Roll as long as I have, the fans become more like extended family—I look out at them at our concerts and I see literally three generations of people who don't necessarily know each other, but know our music… it's truly amazing to me. Their loyalty, energy, and sincerity have kept the whole thing going for all these years and make every show special and fun.

No matter what kind of projects we get involved in—concerts, recordings, my autobiography *Me, the Mob, and the Music*, my radio show on SIRIUS/XM, merchandising, whatever—I know they will be there and have my back.

Our fans are the absolute greatest, and I can't tell you how much I love and appreciate them.

I also can't say enough about Ken Schwartz, who had the terrific idea to write this wonderful book about ROCK N ROLL from the fan's point of view, a long overdue perspective. Ken is the son of Red Schwartz, who in my opinion, was the greatest record business promotion man there ever was and who was one of the most important people in my life and career. God bless you Ken, and all the luck in the world with this great book…. All my best,

Tommy James

Pre

face

"I dig music." *–Russell Hammond, Stillwater,* Almost Famous

No other movie quote quite sums up how I feel about music. It's been with me from day 1–singing "Rhinestone Cowboy" by Glenn Campbell as a very young child in the back of my mom's 1977 "get-out-and-push" Peugeot, to just right now, sitting here, writing this book, and listening to Pantera on my home Alexa device. Yes, the wife is out of the house for a bit–otherwise, it would be playing Fleetwood Mac and Alanis Morrissette, right honey?

Music is a part of everything I've done in my life. From everything I've done well, like adopting two children and teaching them all about AC/DC:

Daughter: "Mommy, daddy taught me all about giving the dog a bone, can I give the dog a treat."

Wife: "Ken–knock that off!"

To some of the worst times in my life–like when my father died, and we had a wake for him playing a lot of amazing classic Latin music, which he loved and which we'll get to later.

But music is always there. In fact, when most people like peace and quiet, I get my peace and quiet from putting on music. To me, peace and quiet means putting on Oasis, Gomez, Travis, Yes, or a million other 'quiet' bands. And when I want to accomplish a task, like cleaning out the office (which the wife has asked me to do for the umpteenth time), I put one some goddam Rock n Roll, like Zeppelin, the Stones, or Pantera.

Oh, side note—Pantera's "Fucking Hostile" just came on, and now I'm typing faster than I ever have in my life. If there was ever a family-snuggle-Christmas-morning-before-church kind of song, this is certainly not it.

RIP Dimebag & Vinnie. Love you, always.

So why did I write this book? I promise you that I didn't write it to brag or to name drop. Although at times, it's certainly going to feel like that. To be honest, I hate people who brag. People who hang out with famous people and then can't shut the fuck up about it. People who show me the same photo of them and ________ (insert famous B-list Hallmark TV movie star here). I've never given a shit who you know, who you got stoned with, or who you saw one day at Ross Dress for Less (OMG is that Sebastian Bach buying khakis?).

But I'm about to do the same thing. I'm about to tell you all the people I've seen at The Cheesecake Factory—all the stories of famous people I know. And I'll use them to tell the story of why I feel music is so important, especially to me in my life.

As you'll read in these pages, I've had a lot of cool experiences in my life. And look, let's be honest—growing up in Southern California, and with a dad who was in the music business for thirty years, I realize I'm a bit luckier than most folks growing up in say, Northern Michigan. Not a lot of star sightings there, unless you count Ted Nugent, and well, frankly, I don't (Just kidding "Nuge"—I love ya, and can listen to "Stranglehold" and "Wang Dang Sweet Poon Tang" on repeat all day long, baby. Well, if the wife is out of the house...).

Despite my many celebrity sightings, I was a shy kid who had no clue how to talk to anyone—especially women—but music got me out of that. When I needed to study for a test, music helped me through it (Hey, that D in Econ didn't earn itself, dammit). When I go on road trips, when I hit the slopes, when I'm pretty much doing anything, I just gotta have those tunes. So, this book is for those of you who feel the same way.

I wrote this book because.... well, simply because *I dig music*... and I wanted to tell you all why, because I bet you dig it too, for a lot of the same reasons. If I'm right, tell me. If you have more reasons, tell me those too. If you hate everything about what I'm about to tell you, why the fuck did you buy the book, dude!?

And one quick note on *Almost Famous*. It's one of my favorite movies of all time, easily near the top of the list. It just simply makes me laugh every time I watch it. Whether I need to waste time on a Saturday night, or had a shitty day at work, this one hits home. Mr. Crowe, I salute thee!

"Oh ok, I'm easy to forget, just leave me behind, I'm only the fucking lead singer...."

Classic stuff. Ok, onward...

Ch
AIN'T
NO
MOUNTAIN
HIGH
ENOUGH

apter 1

"Ain't No Mountain High Enough"

From Diana Ross to Tito Puente: An Introduction to the Music in My Life, and Why I Couldn't Wait to Get Out of the Fucking Car

Music was everywhere growing up in my Southern California apartment complex. Yes, I grew up in West L.A., but on the "wrong side of the tracks", or shall I say, on the "south side of San Vicente" and not in any of those nice houses you all got to know so well years later during the O.J. Simpson debacle.

I grew up in a small two-bedroom apartment on Gorham Ave that cost my parents around $500 a month in rent. It started in the 70's! Now that place is probably going for $2,500 minimum and that just makes me laugh. I wonder if the new residents ever found those toys I left in the holes in the closet wall.

It was a good childhood. No woeful tales of mommy and daddy neglecting me. No horrific moments of despair or desperation. I could always tell money was tight; we had to save for everything, cut back, sacrifice to get something cool, and generally just watch our bottom line.

But I always felt loved. Shit, I was the only child. So frankly, I felt OVER-loved. Leave me alone parents—I'm just reading my comic books. Same place you found me twenty-two minutes ago when you last checked on me! While sweet, this proved exceedingly uncomfortable when I got to my masturbation years—but I'm not sure those stories are going to make it into this book. You're welcome.

I walked to all my schools, rode my bike in the neighborhood, had some cool friends, and generally, just lived life as a normal kid.

But there was always music. Music before and after dinner. Music shows to watch on TV. New records my dad would bring home. Actual vinyls—man, those were epic. He would play me RB Greaves, Kool & the Gang, Celia Cruz, The Temptations, The MC5, KISS, and everything in between. We would try out everything. And then discuss what we liked, and didn't like.

"That one's a bit loud for me and not as soulful as Otis Redding," said Mom.

"This one is going to be a star," said Dad, after playing the first ever KISS album.

"Who are the girls on the cover?" said a three-year-old Ken when looking at Gene, Paul, Peter, and Ace, the only lineup that matters in KISS-land, in my opinion.

And that's how our nights and weekends went. So, all in all, not a bad way to grow up.

But let me tell you a little bit about the people who influenced me so much.

Chapter 1.1

Mom the Hippie

My mom, Pauline, was a '60s hippie with flowers-in-her-hair who had a love for groovy toons, Motown, and dancing in a field without shoes on while certain, shall we say, *pungent* aromas, permeated the atmosphere.

She's hasn't changed, as you can see from her 50th high school reunion photo at the end of the chapter. Peace and love Mum, peace and love.

To this day, Mom can still shake, shake, shake, shake her booty, to some great sounds of the '60s and '70s at her senior citizen workout class in Port Hueneme, California, where she tells me all the time about her music-filled day.

Motown will always be her favorite. The Temptations, Diana Ross, The Jackson 5, etc. She's been playing that stuff since the day I was born, and probably why I love it to this day.

Quick side note about my mother: As I got older, I realized I got my anarchistic, don't-give-a-fuck-but-always-be-polite attitude from her. She's a sharp-witted pistol with a warm embrace in one hand and a dagger in the other. Don't cross her path the wrong way, but if you do, bring wine. And then you'll be her best friend!

Mom has one great famous story in her life. Well, a lot more, but only one I was allowed to print in these pages.

June 16-18, 1967. Mom was just eighteen years old. And the story I heard all my life is that she and her friends decided to pull the old switcheroo with their parents.

"Hey Mom, I'm spending the weekend at Vicki's house."

Vicki: "Hey Mom, I'm spending the weekend at Pauline's house."

Then they hopped in a VW Van with their friends Rita and Marilyn—seriously can this be any more hippie—you might as well have painted flowers on the side of it—and headed north to *The Monterey Pop Festival.*

Simon & Garfunkel, Otis Redding, The Who, Janis Joplin, Jimi Fucking Hendrix! And many others. I mean, holy shit! Just epic.

They just don't do them like this anymore. They've tried (Thanks for fucking it up, Woodstock reunion organizers!). But I'm just not sure they can ever measure up. Lollapalooza tried. Warped Tour was cool for a bit. Mayhem Festival and even OzzFest provided some excellent evenings. But I'm just not sure they'll ever measure up to this, or the original

Woodstock, or even Altamont—you know, before all the death and destruction.

So, Mom and her besties engineered this trip and had three days of listening to the best music ever made, by all the masters who made it. Just dancing (barefoot!) in the sun and grass, meeting new people, sharing great food, and smoking… well, god only knows what they were smoking.

It was a great weekend "at Vicki's house" and they almost got away with it. Almost.

On the way back down from Northern California, Marilyn might have had a bit too much to smoke, fell asleep at the wheel, and rolled the VW Van into a ditch about halfway home.

"Hello, is this Pauline's mom? This is the San Luis Obispo County Sheriff's Department; your daughter Pauline is in the hospital up here and we need you to come get her."

"No sir, that's not possible—she's at Vicki's house for the weekend."

"Um, ma'am, I'm not sure how to tell you this, but she wasn't… please come get her."

Well, let's just say that was the iciest ride home in the history of Highway 101, and Mom was "encouraged" to move out on her own soon after that. She did, to Hollywood, which is where she met my dad, at some discothèque called The Candy Store. I really don't want to know what went on inside those walls.

Looking back, I'm sure Mom felt kind of bad about what she put her parents through. But then again, when she's dancing in her senior Zumba class to Otis Redding or The Byrds, I'm sure she doesn't really care that much! But at the end of the day, that concert got her out of the house, to an independent life, which is where she met my dad, and eventually had me—her greatest creation ever, of course.

B-Sides

Side note about Vicki—who I'm sure also had the same conversations with her parents. Vicki became a fashion model, toured the world, and ended up being the common-law wife of Don Cornelius of Soul Train fame. They were together for more than twenty years and were really cute together. She was even one of those cool 'award-handing-out' gals at the awards show.

"Best Pop Star—Bobby Brown!" and then Vicki would hand them their little trophy and step back while they made their long-winded speeches. Why does everyone make those speeches so long? Anyway.... Vicki is just a delight, still beautiful, and just a lovely person to have in your life.

And pssst—I wanted to sneak in one more story. Don't tell her I added this, but there's also a fun story where my mom went to a party with my dad and ended up sitting on the lap of one of her idols—Barry White, a good friend of my dad's. ("A good friend of my dad's" will be a phrase you hear often in this book. It just is what it is). When it was time to go, Mom was still sitting on the lap of Barry White and didn't want to leave.

She would always tell me, "He just had the sexiest voice I've ever heard, so deep and exciting, and just a super nice man. Hmmm, that was a delicious night."

"Delicious", Mom? Really? I think I'm going to be sick (but I'm glad you had fun... I think).

Chapter 1.2

Dad the Music Man

If you were in the music business in the '50s, '60s, '70s, and early '80s, you were more than likely a friend of Red Schwartz, or Redz. (Redz was his 'east coast nickname', changed to Reds when he moved west. I'm still not sure why, but there you have it.)

Dad knew everybody. From the best musicians of all time, to the people who swept the floors while those people were recording. And to his credit, he treated all of them equally—which I've always respected and tried to follow as an example.

My dad started out as a radio DJ—the only white DJ on an all-black-music oriented radio station WDAS in Philadelphia. He worked something like the one to five shift every night. They had to hide the white guy, I guess!

But Dad's love for 'soul' music—black music and Motown—and his generally-friendly demeanor endeared him to the radio station, where he did quite well for a few years. I have some of his ramblings on a cassette tape somewhere, and it's pretty fun to hear a young Redz talk about the new groove from The 5 Royales, "This is Dedicated to the One I Love," the latest single from The Del-Phis, "My Heart Tells Me So," and even doing commercial breaks for Girard Chevrolet, "where you can find the latest deal on a Chevy Bel Air from the great staff at Girrrrrrrrrrard Chevrolet!" (He would extend those R's forever, and it just cracks me up. Go Dad!)

After yakking it up on the late-night shift for many years, Dad decided he wanted to do more than play the music; he wanted to find the music. He wanted to *be* the music. So, he went to work for a record company, and well, let the adventures begin.

Dad worked for many companies over the years—RCA, Capitol, and he even had his own label for a short time—Red Top Records. Best name ever for a redheaded CEO. They had a few hits. The Quintones, The Ivy-Tones, (was everything a Tone back then?), and The Blue Notes, which brought us Harold Melvin, a legendary soul singer and really nice guy.

He also worked at the famous, or notorious, Roulette Records in New York City.

Dad knew the good people and bad people in the music industry, mingled with the stars who sang the songs, and at Roulette, hung out with some of the mafia who ran the business behind the scenes. In fact, Dad worked there for years under the famous—or infamous—Morris Levy, an alleged member of the Gambino crime family, and an all-around not-very-nice-I'm-gonna-break-your-kneecaps-if-you-don't-sign-this-contract kind of guy.

One of my dad's greatest successes of all times, Tommy James—of Tommy James and the Shondells ("Mony Mony", "Crimson and Clover", "I Think We're Alone Now", "Draggin The Line" and many more)—wrote a great book about these years at Roulette. It's called *Me, the Mob, and the Music* and it's just excellent. My dad is all over it. So, if you want to stop reading this book and go read that one, I'll allow it—but hurry back because things are about to get fun.

As of this writing, Tommy's book is currently being turned into either a Broadway play (as is all the rage these days for Rock n Roll—thanks Jersey Boys) or a movie (as is all the rage these days for rock bio pics, thanks Freddie Mercury and Elton John—both excellent movies, by the way!).

But I know what you're thinking. Redz must've been a total criminal, and that's how I got all these great stories. But this isn't one of those mobster movies about how crime does pay, and my connections came only through the mafia.

No.

I want to set the record straight about this. My dad was not a gangster. He was not mafia. He was not a criminal. He was the most honest straight shooter I ever knew. Did he hand out payola (the practice of paying DJ's to play your record—usually cash, drugs, or women) during his time in the music business? Yes. But did he stop after it became illegal in 1960? Also, yes.

As for the mafia guys—yes, he did know them and did hang with them. Hell, I probably met some of them when I was a young kid too, and just never knew it. And I have very little doubt Dad heard, saw, or knew some things, and never told anyone about them—ever. Not even me.

To put it another way, my dad was doing the 'legitimate business' in the front room. The business that made the books good and the IRS happy, while all the shenanigans were g on behind the closed office doors.

Again, read Tommy's book for a better account of all this. He was there. He lived it and knows the dirt. My dad protected me from all that my entire life, so in this specific area, I've got very few stories to share. Sorry, not sorry.

If you want more, go watch *Goodfellas* or *The Sopranos* and satisfy your urge for mafia stories. In fact, there was a character in the Sopranos, Hesh Rabkin, who was loosely based on Morris Levy from Roulette Records. And the great actor Paul Mazursky played Morris in *Why Do Fools Fall in Love*. Enjoy.

On the other hand, Dad had more music stories than I could ever fit in one book. In fact, to be quite honest, I really wish my dad wrote a book before he passed away in December 2000. He's the one that knew everyone. He was in the recording booths, the DJ booth, and the contract-signing table. He went to the parties, dated famous people, and there's even a rumor he hung out "a little too much" with Lucille Ball. But Dad never got to that, so you get me. Alas.

B-*Sides*:

Just a few more famous Redz stories before we go on:

- Dad swore he signed The Beatles to Roulette Records before anyone had ever heard of them. I do know The Beatles released two songs on Roulette—"Please Please Me," and "Love Me Do"—which sold "just about nothing" as my dad used to say. Roulette sold the contract to Capitol Records, who released the song "I Wanna Hold Your Hand" and well, the rest is history. Curiously enough, within a year or two, Roulette released a full-length Beatles album, and to the day he died, my dad was never sure exactly how that happened, or whose kneecaps had to be broken to get there.

- Early in his music career, my dad became friendly with Diana Ross and the Supremes, Little Richard, and other artists of that era. He even accompanied them on a tour in the early '60s. Back then, a tour consisted of six or seven artists traveling together. They would play three or four hit songs, and get off the stage for the next act to come on. At one point in the tour, along some stop in the south, Dad and the Supremes walked into a diner to get some food after the show. You can imagine what happened next with four black ladies and my very white dad entering a diner in the south in the '60s.

  One note: Please, I beg your forgiveness for the word I'm about to use next. I hate this word. Truly. But it's integral for the story. My apologies! So, Dad and the Supremes walked in and all the heads turned their direction. The lovely-sophisticated-gentlemanly-diner-manager yelled at my dad from behind the counter: "Get out of here, we don't serve niggers here!" To which my dad calmly replied, "That's good, because I don't want to eat a nigger!" (Dad was a bit of a smartass—but still no clue where I got it from). Well, let's just say that didn't go over very well. The lovely-sophisticated-gentlemanly-diner-manager produced a double-barreled shotgun from behind the counter and pointed it straight at my dad's head. Diana and the girls urged my dad to leave and started backing up out the door, but my dad stood his ground and said "Look, I just want to feed the band. Can I please order a couple sandwiches to go and we'll eat them in the hotel room?" Well, I guess the lovely-sophisticated-gentlemanly-diner-manager couldn't pass up a buck, so he took the order, made the food, and put the cash in the old clackety register as Dad hustled out the door back to the hotel.

- My dad loved Latin Music. Eddie Palmieri was an early star for Roulette Records and Dad just loved him—and frankly, the whole genre. He loved it so much, that every weekend when I was young, we'd hang out for a bit, go to eat at McDonalds, or visit my favorite comic book store—Hi De Ho Comics in Santa Monica—and he would force me, like a soldier through the Bataan Death March, to listen to 88.9 KXLU's weekend show *Alma Del Barrio*, the entire ride. While singing in his horrible Spanish, he'd be playing timpani on the steering wheel and windshield wiper switch. Jesus, I couldn't wait to get out of the fucking car. "This isn't Duran Duran, Dad!" I would scream at him, but he didn't care, and just kept singing along. I hated it then, but it was such a great musical education that I just can't get enough of Tito Puente, or Celia Cruz, or the Buena Vista Social Club to this day. Anyway, Dad loved this music so much, he joined something called the L.A. Mambo Society. Years later, he and the whole Society were invited to be extras in the Antonio Banderas movie, *Mambo Kings*. If you have a second, my dad is very easy to spot. In all the dance club scenes, in a giant room filled with amazing and beautiful Latinos and Latinas, there's my dad with white hair, a white mustache, in a white hat and wearing a white suit. Talk about sticking out like a sore thumb. But it's so fun to watch him, even twenty-five years later. He was an amazing dancer, and still looks good on screen in his ridiculous white suit.

- Occasionally, I'm flipping through the music channels in the hopes of actually catching an old video I used to love when I was glued to MTV. No one plays videos anymore, but I'm still hopeful. Once in a while, I stumble across VH1's *Behind the Music*, the story of Alan Freed—the Cleveland radio DJ who is given credit for the term Rock n Roll, and is the main reason the Rock n Roll Hall of Fame was built in Cleveland—and not some city we all want to go to (just kidding Cleveland, Cleveland rocks!). Anyway, my dad knew Alan and is on the VH1 episode. It's really cool to see and hear him long after he passed, but it's spooky too. Imagine flipping around at 1 a.m. trying to find five good minutes of something before nodding off, and suddenly you hear a voice from the past and it's asking you why you didn't do your homework! Well, it's not exactly that, but it's close. Overall, it is cool to see dad on TV now and then.

Chapter 1.3

"Talkin' Bout My Generation"

So, what about my music story? What pieces did I pick up from these two music-loving parents I was lucky enough to be born to?

Well, as you've read, I was never without music in my life. I grew up on all the cool stuff I mentioned above, but started to find my own way in the early '80's.

At that time, I attended an after-school and summer-camp called Phoenix Recreation. It was a cool way to play sports, avoid homework, and otherwise just be a goofy pre-teen in Southern California. We would take road trips all the time to nature parks to look at tadpoles, to museums to learn stuff, and to the Roller Rink on Parthenia Ave! Oh man, did we love the roller rink. Because it had music, right? Nope. Because it had girls? Nope. Because it had video games and I had quarters from my dad? Nailed it.

Yeah, I was kind of a dork back then. ("What do you mean back then?" says every friend reading this book, including my wife!) I guess I was the first generation of kids who got their ya-ya's from a screen. Now, we know it's an epidemic, but back then, it was all brand new—so exciting and so much fun.

During these excursions, did I talk to girls? Of course!

"Hey Jenny, guess who just got the high score on Galaga?"

"Hey Linda, bet you can't beat me at Donkey Kong!"

"Hey Bonnie, that pink dress makes you look just like Ms. Pac Man!"

Yup, when it came to the ladies, it didn't get much smoother than yours truly.

People who know me may never believe this part of the story because now, I never shut the fuck up. These days, I go into a supermarket and ten minutes later, the checkout counter girl and me are having beers and telling stories. Postman? Best friend. Car dealer? Came to my wedding. But back in the '80s and part of the '90s, I couldn't get two words out to a cute girl without totally falling over myself and looking like a complete loser.

Oh, and by the way, I still own the high score in Galaga at the 7-11 in Burbank. Best game ever. Think you can beat me? Bring it!

So, on all these road trips I used to take with Phoenix Recreation, they would also play music. Most of it came from "The Mighty Six Ninety," an AM radio station (XEWW) out of Tijuana, Mexico, that somehow made it all the way up to Los Angeles. Remember, back then, AM radio ruled the roost, and this was the best one of all from what I could tell.

They played Duran Duran, The Thompson Twins, Men at Work, Thomas Dolby, Blondie, and other bands of that day. They often played "I'm on a Mexican Radio" too, by Wall of Voodoo. I always thought that was ironic and funny.

"I wish I was in Tijuana, eating bar-be-que iguana..." So great.

Then at the roller rink, we'd get all this same music, plus cool stuff like Earth, Wind, & Fire, some disco, and a lot of other weird stuff that I would always tap my toes to, while playing video games. Sigh.

With that said, I truly believe my undying love for Donna Summer came from those days in the roller rink. I'm not the biggest disco fan in the world—it had its time and place, and

I'm glad that time was long ago and that place was far away. But don't ever diss my Donna. That girl could flat-out sing. And the songs between her and writer/producer Giorgio Moroder–like "Love to Love You Baby," "Bad Girls," and the crème de la crème, "Hot Stuff," were seared into my musical memory on that roller rink floor–yes, I did skate once in a while–and stayed with me to this day.

"Lookin for some hot stuff baby, this evening..."

Go ahead, try and get that out of your head for the next few chapters. Just great, great shit.

So, I was happy with my musical intake at this time. I had a great upbringing and was finding out what I liked and didn't like amongst my own age group. Men at Work–Yes! Depeche Mode–Hell No. And so on.

And then it all changed.

In the Summer of 1983, my parents saved up for months so my dad and I could go back east and visit all his old friends. Dad was born in Philly and lived in New York, but called L.A. home. He loved the west coast, the people, the weather, the beach, and the Lakers! But he had family back east, and tons of friends from the music business scattered all over, so he took his twelve-year-old son on a trip that changed his musical life.

We set out in June or July of that year and went to New York City (where I almost got lost walking those ridiculous streets) to Philly (where I was forced to eat my bubby's lima bean-filled pot roast) and to DC (where I got to see all the cool monuments I learned about in history class).

And then on to Miami, where we stayed with my dad's buddy, Phil. And Phil had a daughter, Alicia, who was just lovely.

Now, I know what you're thinking. Ken got his first boner in Miami, loved some new band because of Alicia for his entire life, still pines over her, and rues the day he took his first shot at love, which only ended up as a one-sided love affair.

Wrong.

Remember, I had zero game in those days. Less than zero. And to be honest, I was twelve, so I wasn't thinking with that part of my anatomy. Yet.

But what Alicia did has lasted much, much longer. She introduced me to heavy metal. (Wherever you are, I love you Alicia!)

We were sitting in her room one day during the trip, and naturally the subject of music came up.

Ken: "So I really like Men at Work and that new Thompson Twins song is really good. So yeah, what do you like?"

Alicia: "Well those are cool, but have you heard this?"

She then proceeded to pull out an album with a colorful explosion on the cover and dropped the needle on "Rock Rock Til you Drop".

Well, you know those scenes in movies, like *Vertigo*, where the hallway just starts extending and seems to go on forever (I found out that's called a Dolly Zoom!). I swear that's what happened to me in that exact moment. The first power chords, that drumbeat, the kick-into-fucking-overdrive moment at the twenty-seven second mark. HOLY FUCKING SHIT. My brain just melted.

And from that day forward, heavy metal was my life. Book over. The end. Thank you for reading.

But wow, holy shit that was epic.

I listened to the whole album that day, and again the next day.

Alicia, the same age, but with ten times the wisdom (naturally) just kept looking at me with a funny smile, as if to say, 'dude I just fucked your world up, didn't I'? She knew. I knew. Life was different. Life was better. Life was Rock n fucking Roll.

I never really gave up my like for Men at Work and Donna Summer and all the bands that defined me before that fateful day. It's fun to go back and visit them from time to time. Especially now, with all the '80s retro concerts and '80s channels and '80s this and '80s that. It's hard to get away from. But it will never be #1. Sorry, Thomas Dolby, you don't make the cut.

Not sure what happened to Alicia all these years later. We kept in touch via mail for a while. You remember letters, don't you? But we drifted apart and then her dad passed away, and I'm not clear where she went next. I hope she's doing well and teaching her kids about music the way I try to teach mine.

So, the first thing I did when I got back to L.A. was beg my dad to get me that Def Leppard album. Although he worked in a different industry at that point, he still had a lot of music friends and they would send him and me albums all the time.

I wore that vinyl out, playing it almost every day after school. I even had to request a second copy! I have no idea who lived in the apartment next to me, but god I feel so sorry for them, putting up with "Billy's Got a Gun" every night for what felt like an eternity. Meh, they were probably John Denver fans anyway, so fuck 'em.

I found out somehow that Def Leppard was touring that year to support *Pyromania*. Not sure how I found out; there was no internet, and I didn't read the papers. I'm guessing either my dad told me, or I saw a poster at Tower Records—a legendary institution which we shall discuss in detail in a future chapter.

However, I found out, and well, it was a big mistake. I begged my parents, pleaded for them to take me to see the show. Used every 'only child' trick in the book—guilt, love, more guilt, chores, anything—to get them to take me.

My mom could tell I was super excited. My dad could tell I was super excited. So, they discussed the idea of me going to see Def Leppard as my first concert ever. They loved their little red headed pumpkin, as Mom used to call me. How could they deny their baby? They sat me down, looked me in the eye, and said... Fuck the Hell NO!

Well, not really—but that's what it felt like. I was crazy to think they were going to let their twelve-year-old angelic (ahem) son go to one of these loud shows filled with hooligans, druggies, and devious women! Big, fat, fucking NO.

But to my parent's credit, they knew I had the bug. They knew music was it for me. And they knew I couldn't be held back. But they also knew that no way in hell was it going to be metal.

So, because of this, the first three concerts of my life were with my dad. And looking back, they were so goddamn fun.

1. Elton John
2. Classic Rock Review with The Turtles, Junior Walker & the All-Stars, Mitch Ryder and the Detroit Wheels, The Grass Seeds, and Tommy James and the Shondells.
3. Chicago

Ok, this wasn't Def Leppard, or Ratt, or Mötely Crüe, or Judas Priest, or Iron Maiden, or any other band I've now loved for over thirty years, but still not a bad start.

During that first show, I couldn't take my eyes off Elton, and no, not that way. Sheesh. Calm down, reader. He was just such an entertainer. He was all over the place, owning that crowd from the first second. He brought us in, let us breathe, and sent us home happy. Kudos to you, Sir Reg, well done.

This was the I'm Still Standing/Too Low for Zero/I Guess That's Why They Called it the Blues tour, so I got to hear all the cool shit, including "Crocodile Rock", which I know he refuses to play anymore. I was very happy, and Dad knew it.

The Classic Rock Review was cool, but wasn't really my scene. It was great to hang with Tommy, and to be honest, it was cool to see "Happy Together" by the Turtles. They were just great. Junior Walker was a monster with that tenor sax. Holy shit, could he play that thing. The other bands were cool, and I got my first ever backstage experience when we went back to see Tommy and just hang out. They had free soda, candy, and snacks and Dad said I could help myself. Rock n Roll rules, man.

Chicago was amazing. I love horns in my rock music to this day because of that show. I said that to my dad at the time, and he steered me towards all the old Stax/Volt recordings of the '50's with great horn sections, like "Try A Little Tenderness", and songs like that. Just awesome.

So, it was these early shows and experiences that shaped me for a life of Rock n Roll.

B-Sides

Well, I put a few stories for my mom, and a few stories for my dad, so how about a few early stories about me, including one big apology, to just about everyone:

- I went to a music convention with my dad–the National Association of Recording Merchandisers, or NARM, in Century City, CA, I believe. People were hocking their latest music, recording implements, and this brand-new format coming soon, called CD's! I picked up a lot of swag that day, but got to meet a cool guy too. Kevin Cronin, the lead singer of REO Speedwagon, was in the crowd and meeting people. *Hi Infidelity* had just come out, and "Take it on the Run" was climbing the charts. Epic song, great album, and a half-naked chick on the cover! In the middle of all this music madness, I got to shake his hand and tell him that I really loved his new album. Did he say, 'thanks kid", tousle my hair, and walk away? Nope. He stood there with me, despite all the industry dudes vying for his attention, and talked to me. Asked me what grade I was in, my favorite sport, what position I played on the baseball field. And of course, what I wanted to be when I grew up. He was just the coolest, most genuine guy you could ever meet–and super nice to boot. And he was the hottest shit in show business at that exact time. Just amazing. I've never forgotten that, and still love REO to this day. In fact, in a twist of fun irony, my wife happens to be from the same town as them–Springfield, IL. So, a few years ago, I took her to see REO, where, no surprise, she knew every single lyric from every single song. I think this one is going to last, folks!

- Ok, I admit, I'm a bit hesitant to put this second story here. The author of this book really can't be that stupid, can he? A true embarrassment, but I promised you the whole story. Okay, here it goes. Decide for yourself. It was March 23, 1987, and my mom, dad, and I got invited to the first-ever Soul Train Music awards show by my mom's friend Vicki. I was a surly teenager by then, and surely had better things to do than accompany my icky, evil parents to a music show where I didn't know anyone. Just kill me now, why don't you? So, I went along, because they forced me to, and met people, and shook hands with people, but really didn't want to be there (if you couldn't already tell). We walked backstage, and someone yelled out "REDZ SCHWARTZ, YOU SONOFA BITCH." Dad screamed. Mom screamed. And they all hugged and kissed, shook my hand, gave me hugs, and invited us all to sit at their pre-show dinner table with them. Dad was friends with Dionne Warwick from way back in the day, so the stories flowed, drinks were drank, and a good time was had by all. I sat down at one of the chairs, just hoping to eat my food without anyone paying attention to me, when a lovely young lady sits next to me and says hi. I do my usual "HI, I'm Ken, nice to meet you' as my icky, evil parents trained me to do, and she responded with "Hi, I'm Whitney, nice to meet you too." The rest kind of went like this:

Ken: "So are you here to see the show tonight?"
Whitney: "Well, actually I'm doing a song in a bit and had to come early to practice."
Ken: "Oh that's cool, so who else do you want to see tonight?"

Whitney: "Oh I don't know, I'm just really excited to see everyone."
Ken (not really looking at her and eating my food): "So, um, yeah, do you like baseball? I like the Dodgers and I play first base for my team and I really like it, how about you?"
Whitney: "Ha, well a little, I guess. Oh, I've got to go, nice to meet you."
Ken: "Yeah, you too."

And so goes the story of when Ken Schwartz sat a dinner table with the amazing gorgeous talented Whitney Fucking Houston and asked her if she liked baseball.

I mean, seriously. Can you please fucking kill me right now?

One hour later, I'm sitting in the seat next to my parents and she comes on stage and does one of her songs and the crowd goes nuts and I literally must have been seventeen shades of red from sheer embarrassment.

Ken Schwartz, Lady Killer. Sigh

But, the next day, I went to school and told *everyone* I could find that I had dinner with Whitney Houston, naturally, and she talked to me, and we discussed music, and famous people, and sports, and then she went to sing her song on live TV. I'm such an ass. RIP Whitney, you're gone too soon. And I'm so sorry I asked you about fucking baseball.

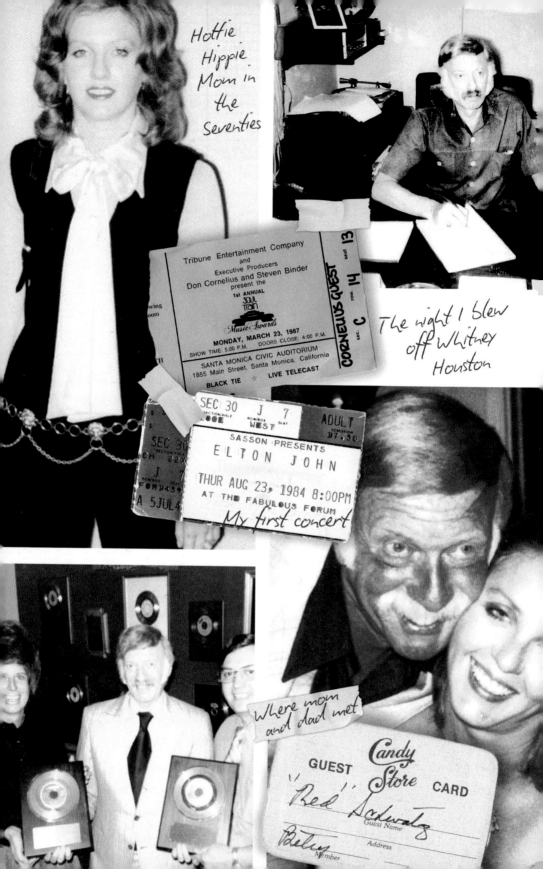

Hottie Hippie Mom in the Seventies
Tribune Entertainment Company
and
Executive Producers
Don Cornelius and Steven Binder
present the
1st ANNUAL
SOUL TRAIN
Music Awards
MONDAY, MARCH 23, 1987
SHOW TIME: 5:00 P.M. DOORS CLOSE: 4:00 P.M.
SANTA MONICA CIVIC AUDITORIUM
1855 Main Street, Santa Monica, California
BLACK TIE ☆ LIVE TELECAST
CORNELIUS GUEST sec. C row. 14 seat 13
The night I blew off Whitney Houston
SEC 30 J 7
SECTION/AISLE ROW/BOX SEAT
LOGE WEST
ADULT
ADMISSION
17.50
SASSON PRESENTS
ELTON JOHN
THUR AUG 23, 1984 8:00PM
AT THE FABULOUS FORUM
My first concert
SEC 30
CH 22X
J 7
A 5JUL4
Where mom and dad met
Candy Store
GUEST CARD
"Red" Schwartz
Guest Name
Address
Member

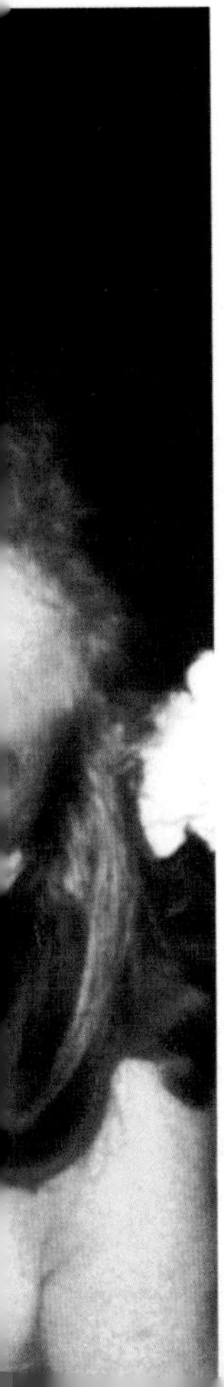

Hottie Hippie Mom Today

Dad with Kool and the Gang

...and he loved telling stories

Ch

LET'S THROW A PARTY. THERE'S A FULL MOON IN THE SKY

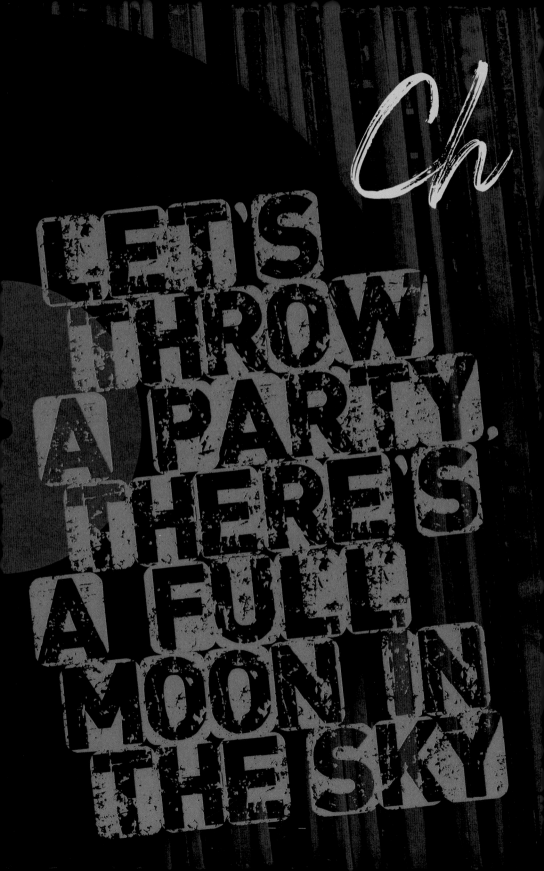

apter 2

"Let's Throw a Party, There's A Full Moon in the Sky"

All Hail Lord Elfman, Free CD's, and Why Music Will Never be the Same Again

So, as you can tell, the '80's were spent with a lot of great music: '80's Pop, '60's Soul, a little bit of Barry White, Latin music, and my new love for heavy metal.

If my dad didn't get them for me for free, then I bought ALL the albums: *Pyromania* (twice!), *Hysteria*, *Appetite for Destruction*, *Out of the Cellar*, *Slippery When Wet*, *Long Cold Winter*, *Love at First Sting*, *Shout at the Devil*, and so many more.

Then, at the age of fifteen and a half plus a day—the legal timeframe to do this in Southern California, and man, did I want it badly—I got my goddam driver's license, and my car had a cassette player! So naturally, I had to re-buy all those great albums on cassette so I could blast them in my car while cruising the 1.1 miles to my school and back. Essentially, about half a song! But it sounded so good when I pulled into the parking lot at Uni High in West L.A. in my powder blue 1986 Ford Courier pick-up truck with racing stripes on the side, a camper shell on the back, and carpet—yes, carpet—in the bed of the truck.

When I turned into that lot blasting "She's got the looks that killlllllllllll," I felt like a fucking god. Everyone else felt like I was a fucking loser, and they probably weren't wrong, but despite all my insecurities, I got my first taste of not really giving a shit about what anyone thought. I'm not going to lie—it took many, *many* more years for that feeling to be dominant in my life. But it started to change, and it started right there in that powder blue truck—and that makes me smile.

Then, a year later, when I turned that truck into an "accordion" because I was playing air drums to The Doors on Melrose Ave and not watching who was stopping in front of me (sorry whoever you were!), I got another car, which—gasp—had a CD player. Well that's cool, I guess. So, I had to get all those great tunes again, but this time on CD!

No, I didn't empty my bank account to do this, and no I didn't do it all in one fell swoop. I had a job, dammit. I waited tables at Chin Chin, a trendy Chinese-American restaurant chain that served really great chicken salads, some pretty strong Bao, and chocolate-covered fortune cookies, which, even though sounds very "L.A.," were actually pretty darn tasty. And they were also so easy to give away to just about every cute chick that sat in my section. I even put my phone number in one once as "the fortune" only to hear raucous laughter coming from Table Twelve some ten seconds after I stepped away from it. At least they left me a nice tip.

I made decent money, lived at home, had no bills, and basically just grew my bank account and bought music. And where does a sixteen-year-old kid with money in his pocket go to buy all this music? There was only one magical, legendary place.

Tower Records was where god himself went to shop for music. And c'mon, if there is a god, and I'm not saying there is, but if there is, he's not listening to the harp or the lute. He's having a fucking shot of Jack with Ronnie James Dio, god dammit (oops, sorry god!). At least that's my take. Anyway, back to Tower.

The place was fucking legendary. Many of you probably already know all about Tower, so I won't dwell on it, but I spent so much time and money there they really should have sent me a Christmas fruit basket for about five straight years.

Albums, Cassettes, CD's, T-shirts, Pins, and Cassingles!

Remember Cassingles? Those things were great! One song, over and over. With some B-side you listened to just because once you were done, it went back to the A-side and you could jam all over again. Plus, it means you didn't have to buy the whole damn tape if you didn't want to. For example, I didn't want the entire album by Biz Markie; I just wanted to get one song so I could drive into the Uni parking lot again and sing:

"Oh baby, youuuuuu, you got what I neeeeeeeed

But you say he's just a friend, yeah you say he's just a friend

OH BABY YOU......"

Come on, that shit was great! (Don't tell anyone, but I think I still have that cassingle in a box in my attic. I just could never get rid of it. Mad respect, Biz!)

The other great thing about Tower Records were the concert tickets. Those of you reading this book who grew up just clicking for concert tickets on their smartphone will just never understand the scene at Tower Records when a big band was coming to town.

Spring 1989:

"Holy shit, did you hear? The Rolling Stones are playing the L.A. Coliseum, with Living Colour, and Guns and Fucking Roses?"

That was all anyone could talk about all summer. Everyone wanted to go. And even though the L.A. Coliseum could hold almost seventy-nine thousand people, not everyone in L.A. was going to get a ticket.

And I wanted a fucking ticket!

So, on the day tickets were to go on sale, I got to Tower Records at five in the morning on a Saturday (after waiting tables 'til about midnight Friday!).

I wasn't even close to first in line. Some people got there at four. And I stood in line for four hours so that I would be one of the first! One of the first people in my neighborhood to be lucky enough, to be honored enough, to be stoked enough, to get a ticket?

Nope, to get a fucking wristband.

Which had a number on it.

Which may or may not be called.

So that I could get back in line and have a chance to get tickets.

Maybe.

Utter fucking madness.

But I wanted to see that show. And no wristband number-calling-Tower-clerk was going to deny me.

Buying tickets at Tower was an event. Your friends were there. Girls were there. You built your whole weekend around it. People sold breakfast burritos. Soda. Drugs. Bootleg T-shirts. Bands handed out flyers to their local shows. Street preachers warned us against our sins of Rock n Roll. It was fucking epic, and it was never boring.

So roughly five-hundred of us got wristbands that morning for the big show. After we all got wristbands, we waited. We mingled. We drank. We smoked. We fought. We joked. We lived. For about an hour, we just waited. Waited for them to call a number. That was the wristband number they were going to start with.

They handed out about five hundred wristbands: one... two... three... five hundred. Then an hour later, someone would come out of the front door of Tower.

The crowd hushed and moved forward. All conversations stopped. People put their sodas down, their breakfast burritos back in their pocket, and threw their gum in the trash. No distractions!

Here came the call. That wristband number-calling-Tower-clerk had so much fucking power and he knew it. Here it was....

"Two Hundred and Thirty-Five—LINE UP"

Fuck. Well, cool. But Fuck.

I was #288.

So that means I was about fiftieth in line—and not guaranteed a shot at tickets. Remember, this same gathering of Rock n Roll knuckleheads was happening at all hundred-plus Tower Records store locations across Southern California!

But I was better off than my buddy, who had #225. Even though his number was 'at the beginning', he ended up at the end of the line. He didn't have a chance. He looked for someone to get him a ticket, begged someone to help him out, and even offered to pay twenty dollars extra just to get in the building. Sorry buddy—go home and go back to bed.

Time to sell the tickets. One person. At a computer. Printing out the old tickets on a dot matrix printer, or so it seemed. It took forever. But there was no Internet then, so it took the same long-ass time at each of those hundred-plus locations.

I stood in line, watching everyone in front of me begging for the line to move quickly.

"Do you have seats in a better section? We don't like these," asked one pair of fucking morons who should have been beaten to a pulp. Don't pick your section! Just get two tickets and get the fuck out of the way so more of us have a chance to get seats. Assholes. Ticket buying etiquette man, come on!

Oh shit, I'm tenth in line. Will there be seats left?

Fifth in line. They're still printing out of the machine.

Shit, I'm next.

I'm up.

"I'll take just one please" as I plopped down my tip money—mostly ones, but occasionally a five if I waited on a large party.

I had a strategy!

You see, if people bought tickets in pairs, and threes, and fours, and fives, there just might, maybe, be *one* seat way down close, and I was going to get that goddam seat. I was going to throw my metal horns up at Axl, and Keith, and Vernon, and they were going to look at me, and throw them right back. And that's how my night was going to go, god dammit.

I paid my fee, took my ticket, and went over to the board to find my seats, so the next person behind me could step up and get some. See, ticket etiquette. Take that, assholes.

I was so excited as the couple moved in front of me and I got to the map. Holy shit where was I sitting?

Oh my god.

Is this for real?

I can't be this lucky.

I was in the second row...the second fucking row....

From the back.

Well, shit.

I sat there staring at the map and started cracking up. I couldn't believe it. I tried to 'play' the system and I got crushed. But whatever. Not even five minutes later, they sold out. Fuck it. I was in the building.

And thus, on October 15, 1989, I drove down to the L.A. Coliseum, in my crappy piece of shit 1980 Mustang with the ceiling interior literally hanging down from the roof of the car, and I saw Living Colour, an amazing live band, Guns N Fucking Roses for the first of many, many times, and the legends themselves, the goddam Rolling Stones, from my second to last, one-person-behind-me-and-I-was-at-the-top-of-the-stadium-seats, and I didn't care one bit because it fucking rocked my world.

Thank you, Tower Records, for helping to make it all happen.

B-Sides

- If you haven't seen it, there is an amazing documentary on Tower Records called *All Things Must Pass*, directed by Colin Hanks—the son of Tom Hanks. It's fantastic, and does an incredible job of capturing the power and spirt of this wonderful institution. I highly recommend.
- And apparently, there are still a few Tower Records floating around, if you know where to look. They have some

in Japan, something about selling the license to a Japanese company. Apparently, they are still big there too. And they have at least one in Dublin, Ireland because I've been there. I was walking with my soon-to-be-wife and talking about our future and our plans and our kids and really deep important shit and then poof... all of a sudden, like mid-sentence, I turned left down this one street because I saw the familiar yellow sign that I swore said Tower Records. And guess what, it did! The wife-to-be grumbled something at me but went into the store and had a blast! I think I went there three times that trip—not exactly what my wife-to-be had in mind for our vacation I'm sure, but she knew what she was getting into when she said yes to marrying me! Love you, honey.

Chapter 21

"Pay to Write, Pay to Play, Pay to Cum, Pay to Fight!"

Up until this point in my life, I listened to what the radio told me to listen to. If the "Mighty Six Ninety" or "KIIS FM" or "Pirate Radio" played it thirty-seven times a day, then who was I to argue? But when I got to college, that all began to change.

My college years were just like everyone's, I suppose. Despite applying to numerous colleges nationwide, and some big colleges locally, I either didn't get accepted to the ones I really wanted, or couldn't afford the ones that said yes. So, I ended up going to college not far from home at California State University, Northridge, or CSUN, where I moved into an off-campus apartment, on Prairie Ave, with my buddy from high school, Ryder.

Ryder was a cool dude. Super smart, and damn good looking. Took me to all his frat parties. Bought me beer. And was way more worldly than I was, because he was a whole one year ahead of me in college, and that was just the best currency anyone could have.

Ryder also had some sick, awesome, amazing, fantastic, and fucked-up taste in music. I mean, just bat shit nuts. And I loved it.

We would have "battles" about music.

We didn't argue, we challenged each other. We would do this before we went 'out' for the night. Some frat party, club, double date, or whatever. I would play the shit I knew and tell him why "Mr. Brownstone" was the coolest song on *Appetite* because of the subject matter. Ryder would say that "It's So Easy" was better because it had the best heavy metal lyric of the '80's.

"You get nothin' for nothin'
If that's what you do
Turn around bitch I got a use for you
Besides, you ain't got nothing better to do
And I'm bored"

Fuck you, Shakespeare, this is REAL poetry, baby!

But Ryder was right.

Then he would start playing some of his sick, awesome, amazing, fantastic and fucked-up music. He played me Metallica's "Kill em All", before any radio station did (if they ever did at all). He played me The Sugarcubes, including some songs in Icelandic! What the hell is a Bjork? ("Birthday" in Icelandic is still so fucking good). The Pixies "Surfer Rosa" was never far from the CD player. And man, did he love Bad Brains! Just a crazy punk band from D.C.–legends. But totally out of this world. I can still hear them screaming "Pay to Cum" through my cheap college sound-system turntable.

It was about this time I started realizing that music didn't have to be what the radio stations were shoveling down my throat. That those *other* aisles at Tower Records, the ones that did NOT have Bon Jovi, Alice Cooper, or Madonna, had something to say—and that I should start checking them out some day. This was some good music. And thanks to these bands, these new tracks, and this time in my life, I still like some weird shit to this day. In fact, I'm going to go put some on right now, just as soon as this Madonna song is over.

"Get into the grooooove..."

Chapter 2.3

"All I Wanna Do, Is Have Some Fun"

So, what did I want to be when I grew up, you ask?

I wanted to be in the record business! No. I wanted to sign bands and own the record business.

I guess the apple didn't fall far from the tree in this area. Dad signed the Beatles. Dad signed Tommy James and the Shondells. Dad worked with Kool & and the Gang and Curtis Mayfield. Well, I was going to do that too! I was going to help define the sound with the bands from my era.

So, I told this all to "Redz" one day. I figured he'd be delighted. He'd laugh and cry and embrace me and the sun would shine, and the clouds would open (as if they actually allowed clouds in Southern California) and all would be well with the world.

Instead, he turned to me and said, "What the hell do you know about the record business?" And then just let that hang there.

Stunned, I had to think on my feet. I'd been to at least twn concerts by that point, and I listened to music all the time. I loved Russell the Love Muscle on Pirate Radio and Jim Ladd on KLOS so yeah, I pretty much knew everything about the music business, Pops—so stuff it.

I didn't know shit.

So, my dad did two things for me that day. Two of the last, but most important things he ever did for my career and me.

One, he bought me what is possibly the greatest music industry book of all time—Donald Passman's *All You Need to Know About the Music Business.*

Just amazing—contract deals, where to record, how to promote—just everything you ever wanted to know about the actual business side of music.

The second thing he did was call up his old friend, Jerry Moss (just another "friend of Dad"). Jerry Moss was the "M" in A&M Records, with Herb Alpert as the "A". Jerry was a music business legend and Dad wanted me to learn from him.

So, during my senior year in college at CSUN, I interned (read: no money) at A&M Records at the beautiful former Charlie Chaplin studios in Hollywood, California shown in the photos at the end of this chapter.

I was on my way to dominating the music business! I wanted to sit in on every meeting, and listen to bands before saying "Yes" or "No" with my thumb like Joaquin Phoenix in *Gladiator*, soaking it all in. My first job for the first few months I was there was....

... stuffing envelopes to put in the mail and send to record stations.

Okay, not exactly what I had in mind.

Keep in mind, this was all happening in the pre-digital era. We couldn't just "Snap-Face" some jpeg/gif/wav sound file to someone's Beats headphone and say, "rock on, dude." We had actual CD's that we put in actual envelopes and sent via the actual post office to all three-hundred or so rock, R&B, or alternative outlets around the country—and we had to do it all day long.

I'm not going to lie—it was fun as hell. And while I was on the floor, or in the conference room, I was listening, watching, and learning not only from the VP's, but also from the real people who got shit done around there: the assistants. They knew where the bodies were buried, and they were the best people to get to know and learn from the entire year I was there.

The other cool part about this internship was that I didn't get paid.

Wait, what did he say?

Yeah, okay, it sucked not getting paid, and I had to keep my job at Chin Chin to make ends meet and pay my ridiculously over-priced college apartment rent of $325 a month, or something like that.

But the cool part was that all the VPs and assistants knew I wasn't getting paid. So, they made up for it in music.

I got to continue my 'fuck radio' music education at A&M Records. I would get a new CD almost every day. Something they were promoting on the radio (after stuffing three-hundred Gin Blossoms CD's into jiffy bag envelopes, they fucking better give me one!) or CD's people sent them that they didn't want. I even got two box sets from The Police for Christmas that year and gave one to my new roommate. You're welcome, Todd.

I got a lot of music that year—Monster Magnet (who I still can't get enough of), Swervedriver, Motocaster, Sheryl Crow's legendary debut CD, The Replacements, Ned's Atomic Dustbin (Ok, look I didn't say they were all *good* CD's!) and so much more.

I will brag here for one second: I was given two CD's during my time at A&M that I totally remember. Not because they were great—they were—but because I knew they'd become big stars—which they did, only furthering my desire to get out of the mail-stuffing room and own the music business myself.

A few months before they broke, I was given a CD copy of *Dookie* by Green Day, and *Cracked Rear View*, by Hootie and the Blowfish. Both of those discs blew my mind, and I remember telling everyone I worked with—by this time at The Cheesecake Factory—that these two groups were going to be huge. I vaguely remember someone telling me to shut the fuck up about Green Day already and go fill iced tea on table 14. Anyway, the world wasn't just filled with Ned's Atomic Dustbin; I got to rock out to some pretty cool shit too.

Not only did I get music I've never heard of that wasn't even played on the radio, but I got a crap ton of concert tickets too. I got sent to every hole-in-the-wall, Sunset club, college gym, and stadium in the L.A. area to see bands. They handed me tickets all the time, and they wanted my opinion of the shows. I had a voice—a small one, but I had one. Still some of the best shows of my life were Damn the Machine at Dragonfly, or Therapy? at the Roxy.

Not sure whatever happened to Therapy? But a heavy metal electric stand-up viola? Sign me the fuck up!

"My girlfriend says.
That I need help.
My boyfriend says.
I'd be better off dead."

Awesome. Love those guys.

There were so many cool shows and too many to mention here, but I will mention one. One that still makes me shake my head and smile to this day.

I got to go see Monster Magnet at the world-famous L.A. Troubadour on Santa Monica Blvd in Los Angeles.

I was all kinds of excited; I couldn't wait to see these guys. *Dopes to Infinity* had just come out (a good CD, but *Powertrip* is much better, in my opinion) and that CD didn't leave my third car—my new baby blue (what is it with me and baby blue?) piece of shit Ford Escort—that entire year.

I was so stoked to see these guys that I got there about two hours early—which is so Un-L.A. Still learning how to be cool, guys.

Anyway, I got there and I was having a cheap house beer because, you know, I had no money, and this crazy opening act comes on stage. Tall white guy with long dirty blonde hair, and a midget next to him (Are you supposed to say midget? Dwarf? Little person? Fuck, I have no idea.). Both were wearing matching purple velour tracksuits and purple Kangol hats. Read that sentence again. Even for L.A., that was just weird. And they started to rap, with a full metal band behind them. Blew. Me. Away.

Well, they totally rocked it—or, rapped it, whatever. And by the end of the show, Kid Rock and Joe C. had totally won over the heavy metal dirtbag crowd that was there to see Monster Magnet. I'm not sure how that tour came together. Some weird amalgamation of rock, country, rap, and matching purple velour track suits with purple Kangol hats, but it worked, and it worked well.

It took a few more years for Kid Rock to break. I think his first hit was in 1998. But he was grinding it out on that stage with Monster Magnet in 1994, and it was a lot of fun to see.

It was a very good year to learn about new music; it really opened my eyes. I started finding radio stations like KROQ, which used to be good and alternative, to 91X (XETRA-FM) out of Tijuana/San Diego, that also played some cool alternative tunes.

And no longer did I have a problem driving in my car and dropping in my Motocaster CD right after I was done listening to *Mandy* by Barry Manilow.

Hey! Fuck you. That guy could totally write the songs that made the whole world sing. Love that shit.

B-Sides:

A few more quick stories from a great year at A&M:

- One of the assistants was the legendary comedienne, Cheri Oteri. She was doing comedy at night with The Groundlings and making a name for herself before heading off to a stellar career on Saturday Night Live and other TV and movies. But before that, this was her day job, and she was brilliant. And funny as shit. And she would show us videos of her comedy skits all the time. If you ever get a chance to find her skit "Super Botanist"—watch it. I still pee my pants thinking about it.

- One of my bosses gave me a note and told me to run it over to the Production Team ASAP! So I got up, and sprinted across the lot to the production area. I ran across the parking spaces at full speed, leaping up the stairs, probably taking four at a time. I got to the very top of the steps… and *literally* ran headfirst into all four members of Soundgarden, who were just leaving some sort of session. Kim Thayil and Ben Shepard looked like they wanted to crush my puny skull with their metal-god hands. I slinked back down the stairs and let them pass. I think I even managed to let out a small whimper that sounded like "sorry guys, and I really love *Superunknown*" but that may have all been in my head. Alas.
- The people I worked with knew I really wanted to get into A&R—or Artists and Repertoire. Basically, the side of the business that actively searches for and signs new bands. They hooked me up with a co-worker named Emily and once or twice a week, we would sit in her office, eat lunch together, and go thru the myriad of packages from "the next big thing" that bands would send us from all over the world. We literally gave every one of those a spin, so for those of you who submitted a song in 1994-1995 to A&M Records, I got to listen to it, judge it, and eventually, reject it. Sorry! Most of them were so awful. But that was a real fun time, doing what I always wanted to do.
    - » Two quick side notes about Emily—after listening to about ten submissions, she would pause and put on, what she called "some really good music to help clear our heads." We put on Zeppelin and all the classics, but also tried some new shit like a band from the desert, called Kyuss. Mind. Fucking. Blown. Then we went back to the brother-sister electric accordion players doing a cover of White Room who thought they were the shit! Sigh. The other story—and one

big goof during that time... we listened to Beck's first-ever submission. I think we laughed at it. I think I said, 'what the hell, no one will ever listen to this clown.' So yeah, Ken Schwartz, intern-extraordinaire, the guy who wanted nothing more than to find new talent and rule the music business, turned down a legendary performer and artist like Beck. Oops, sorry, Emily!

Chapter 2.4

"This is Not a Cat Show, With Prizes at the Door"

My penultimate experience with new, odd, fuck-you-radio type music came in the form of Oingo Boingo. Originally called The Mystic Knights of the Oingo Boingo in the 70s, this band RULED the SoCal music scene in the late '80's and early '90's.

This part of the chapter is going to be a little weird. If you were anywhere near Southern California, in these years, you had zero choice but to know Oingo Boingo. KROQ never stopped playing them. They always played shows, usually doing a week of shows around July 4th and a week of shows around Halloween. All the wannabe surfer kids like me loved them.

If you grew up anywhere else, you probably just know them from that one Rodney Dangerfield/"guy who plays Iron Man" movie, *Back to School*, where they were the house band, or from the theme song to the movie *Weird Science*, or their one hit that went nationwide that you hear every Halloween, "Dead Man's Party".

It's a Dead Man's Party
Who could ask for more?
Everybody's comin'
Leave your body at the door
Leave your body and soul at the door.

If you lived in SoCal, you get it. If you didn't, you won't.

If you wanted to party, dance, meet members of the opposite sex, or the ultimate good time, you went to an Oingo Boingo show. I imagine this is what New Yorkers said when first seeing Patti Smith or The Ramones at CBGBs, or what Brits said when The Clash first played The Marquee Club in London. It was just something you had to see.

Led by the overly energetic Danny Elfman, Oingo Boingo was a party in a can. (Yes, this is the same Danny Elfman who now scores movies for Tim Burton and others. He left Boingo behind to do this, and while I was pissed at the time, I totally get it, and his movie scores are epic. Don't believe me? Go listen to—not watch—listen to *The Nightmare Before Christmas*. Just fucking amazing.)

Boingo had a full band with an epic horn section, two keyboard players, and one of the craziest motherfuckers on drums of all time, Johnny Vatos. That dude was the timekeeper on those skins, and one of the oddest guys you'll ever see. And I was 'this close' to getting a Johnny Vatos signature pink mohawk until my friends talked me out of it. But anyway...

Boingo even had one song with a double xylophone solo. Okay, it's kind of cool when a band introduces some new ideas into a song. Jimmy Page and his legendary violin bow. Therapy? and the electric viola. Hell, even Tiny Tim and his fucking guitar on "Tiptoe Though the Tulips!" But not one, two xylophones on one song, live on stage, in front of thirty thousand people was just insane. And when Boingo kicked off the first chords of their song "Grey Matter", the crowd knew they were in for a treat.

I was lucky enough to see Boingo thirteen times in my life. Probably one 4th of July show and one Halloween show for five years in a row, and their grand finale show at the (formerly called) Universal Amphitheatre on or around Halloween, 1995. They put out a good double CD from this show called *Farewell*. I listen to it all the time, because I like weird shit, remember?

I don't think I do Boingo justice in this part of the chapter; I don't think it's possible to relay the power and amazement and just pure joy they brought to music in those years. The fun had by all, and the great songs punctuated by the epic drumming from Mr. Vatos. It's just too hard to describe to you if you didn't live through it. I hope I did okay. But you know what I think—I think they need to play again. Everyone is doing reunion tours (looking at you Motley Crüe!) So why not Boingo? What say you, Mr. Elfman?

But this section isn't just about Boingo. It's that local band that not everyone knows nationwide, but for you, locally, they're your whole life for a short period of time. In the upper Midwest, in the '90s it was the Gear Daddies. In D.C., it's Chuck Brown and Go-Go music. Mid-coast, probably Dave Matthews before he got super famous.

It's about that local phenomenon that creates community. The one you still talk about with your friends to this day.

You likely have your own. Tell us, who is it, and where can I find their CD?

B-Sides

- A friend of mine from The Cheesecake Factory actually won free tickets to that Oingo Boingo Farewell show and after weeks of me begging her, she took me with her... and then charged me for the free ticket! (Concert etiquette people, come on!) Well I wanted to get inside that damn show and say goodbye to the ultimate party band. So, I met her at the Amphitheater and gave her a hug, a big smile, and a check for thirty-five dollars. I saw the show, rocked my ass off, went home, called Bank of America, and cancelled the check. Do I feel badly about this? Meh. Depends on the day. But don't charge people for your free ticket—that's just lame.

Tower. Dublin.
Feb. 2019

Lady killer in training!

The legendary Tower on Sunset - Take my money please!

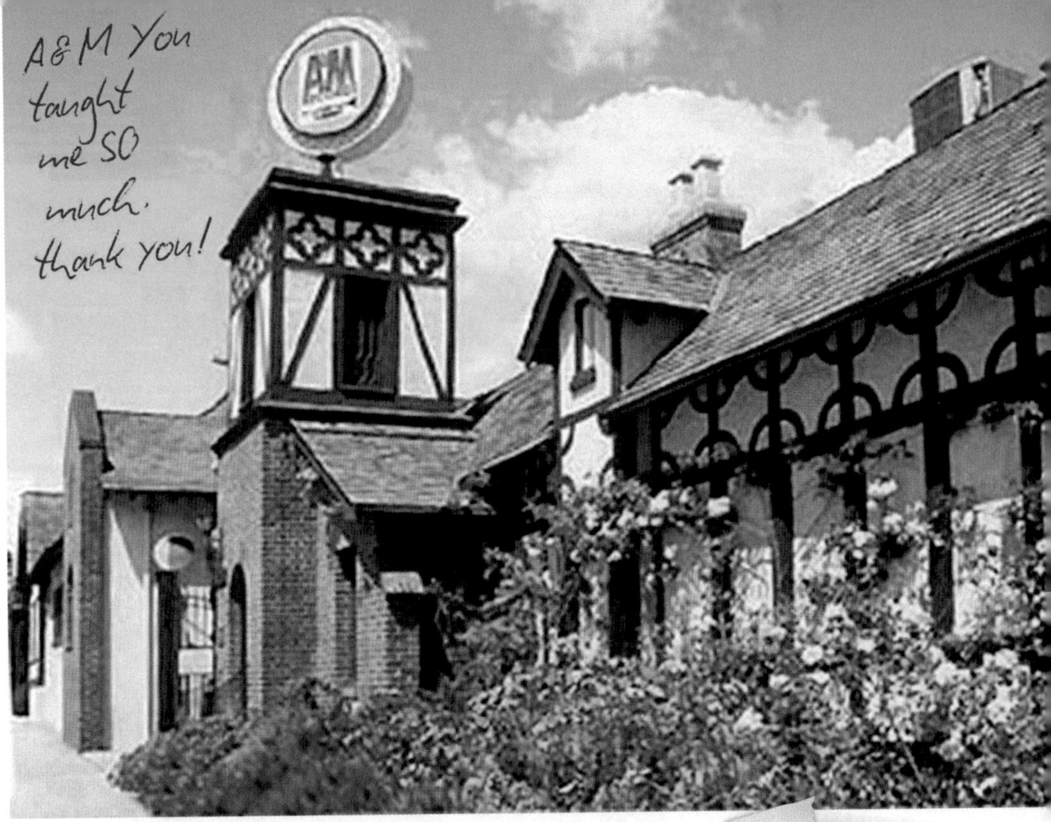
A&M You taught me SO much. thank you!
A&M

PIRATE RADI
100.3

SEC 10 6 102
TUNNEL 10 SOUTH
MTV PRESEN
THE ROLLING S
RAIN/SHINE*NO CAM
GUNS N' ROSE
LOS ANGELES COL
SUN OCT 22, 1989
THE UNIVERSAL AMPHITH
PRESENTS
** OINGO BOINGO **
NO REFUNDS NO EXCHAN
FRI JUN 30, 1989 8:15

"The industry bible." –Los Angeles Times
ALL YOU NEED TO KNOW
ABOUT THE
MUSIC
BUSINESS
HOW STREAMING has radically restructured the music business
UPDATES ON HIGH-PROFILE copyright infringement cases
THE MUSIC MODERNIZATION ACT and what it means to the industry
10th Edition
DONALD S. PASSMAN

Best live party band everrrr

Ch

WELL, LET ME WELCOME EVERYBODY TO THE WILD, WILD WEST

apter 3

"Well Let Me Welcome Everybody to the Wild, Wild West"

Two White Boys in Cowboy Boots Bouncing to Ice Cube on the Sunset Strip, and Why Early Rap Will Always Be the Best

When I wasn't throwing up my metal horns in the car while screaming "she's a rainbow in the daaaaaaark...." or bopping my head to some Michael Jackson, because that's what all the girls liked, and I liked all the girls, there was another curious thing happening at this time that took all of music in a different direction.

Love it or hate it, rap became, and still is, a force in the musical world. You couldn't escape it. It was brand new, exciting, and it was everywhere.

Picture for a second, a scrawny six-foot tall kid, barely one-hundred-fifty pounds, with a giant Q-tip of orange hair doing whatever the hell it wanted on his head, who grew up in an apartment in a pretty affluent (read: mostly white) neighborhood in West L.A., listening to Run-DMC for the first time.

> *"You know I'm proud to be black y'all*
> *And that's a fact y'all*
> *And if you try to take what's mine*
> *I take it back y'all... it's like that..."*

Wait a second. This didn't have a verse-chorus-verse set up or a wailing guitar solo or monster drum fill. This was different.

That young scrawny kid stood in the schoolyard and said: "Wow, is this what's really going on in those parts of the city I've never been to? Not once, not ever."

I just assumed it was.

My first true exposure to this new art form happened on the bus. Not the bus to and from school, but the baseball bus. I was a back-up-never-got-off-the-bench first baseman for the Uni High Junior Varsity baseball team. The same team I made sure to tell Whitney Houston all about. Sigh.

Baseball was (and is) my favorite sport, but I was just plain bad at it. Much better coach than player, my friends would always tell me. I think I went one for eleven in my *entire* high school baseball career. Batted .091 baby. Look out Yankees–here I come.

The one cool thing about those days was getting on the bus to go play away games at Venice High, Palisades High, or Westchester High, etc. That's when the fun happened.

Every time we got on that bus, for two straight seasons, we listened to *Raisin' Hell* by Run-DMC, *License to Ill*, by The Beastie Boys, and of course, Eddie Murphy's *Delirious*, because it allowed us to swear–a lot.

"You don't have no ice cream, cuz you are on the welfare. Want a lick? Psyche!"

Fucking brilliant.

But it was on that bus where we had our rap 'battles'. One side of the bus would be Run, the other side would be DMC. Or, one side would be MCA, and the other would be Mike D. Round and round we'd go.

Maybe if I put as much effort into swinging a baseball bat, as I did into memorizing those rap lyrics, I might have had an actual shot at batting over .100. Probably not, but we'll never know!

But this is a time in my life that helped open my eyes to music that had absolutely nothing to do with me. I never lived this life. And frankly, I wasn't always sure what the hell they were talking about.

Yes, I had friends of all colors. That never mattered to me, and still doesn't. But we all grew up in West L.A., so, to be honest, they didn't have that kind of life either. The kind we heard on those early to mid-'80s rap records.

I wanted to know more.

I started listening to anything I could find, trying out different L.A. radio stations that were brave enough to play this new art form. I begged my dad for rap albums from his music friends, and also bought all the new rap I could find (especially on cassingle!). And I even got to meet 2 Live Crew at that same convention where I met the lead singer of REO Speedwagon. They were totally cool dudes, who apparently were very, very horny and loved everyone "long time."

I bought everything I could get my hands on: Public Enemy, EPMD, Eric B. & Rakim, Salt N Pepa, The Fat Boys, 2 Live Crew, and eventually NWA. And so much more.

I wanted to go to rap concerts and be 'in the scene.' This was about the same time I was dying to go to heavy metal shows, so if my parents said no to those, they sure as hell weren't going to say yes to rap concerts either.

Going to a rap show didn't happen for quite a while. It was many years before I saw my first one, The Beastie Boys, and that was at Lollapalooza in 1994. There were a couple reasons for this. One was that rap shows really didn't come around that often. Or if they did, I didn't hear about them. Perhaps I was looking in the wrong place. I read the LA *Weekly* all the time—the best spot for concert announcements before the Internet, and never saw them advertised. Was there a rap version of the LA *Weekly* that I missed? I don't know.

The second reason is that there was also a lot of violence at rap concerts. Gang fights, fist fights, shootings, and other shenanigans always seemed to dominate the news cycle. It was sad to hear about. It took away from the artist, their art form, and what they were trying to say. And it certainly kept away kids like me that wanted nothing to do with those sorts of situations—and all the parents of those kids too.

But early rap definitely found a place inside my heart: the beats, the clothes, and the message all made me who I am. No, I didn't come to school in a purple velour track suit and Kangol hat—that would have been so tragic if I tried—but I sure thought about it. The rap music of that era had so much to say, so much to teach people, and so many doors to open. It was revolutionary.

And then it changed.

Out of nowhere, literally overnight, it seemed that rap become all about 'bitches and money, yo."

And rap got bad.

I didn't want to hear about young kids throwing money at strippers. I didn't want to hear about them "rolling in their Benzes". I don't care if 'your man paid for the rent.'

What the hell was this?

Rap became intolerable. Not worth listening to and not worth buying. I still listened for nuggets here and there. Some new rapper who harkened back to the 'old' days of a few years ago, but those were few and far between. So, I went back to what I knew—to my old friends on vinyl, cassette, and CD. I tuned rap out for many years while this was going on, except for maybe the occasional night on the dance floor.

And look, I put this all on me. These new rappers, these kids had every right to sing about "bitches and money, yo" if they wanted to. They earned it; they were allowed to be rich. They were allowed to meet nice ladies and ask them on a date to Ye Olde Faire or a pleasant walk along the lake. They were allowed to be happy in their fine Mercedes automobiles.

I just didn't care; it didn't speak to me the way the earlier stuff did. It didn't make me curious or want to know more. So instead, I tuned it out and went back to Rock n Roll 100% of the time.

And then came Snoop D-O-Double-G.

Chapter 3.1

"Where My Dogs At?"

Snoop dropped his epic CD, *Doggystyle*, in 1993 and debuted at #1 on the Billboard 200 charts, which surprised the hell out of everyone. The CD sold over 800,000 units in the first week, was eventually certified four times Platinum, and had two killer cross-over singles that even got played on my alternative and Rock n Roll stations, "What's My Name", and "Gin & Juice".

No one saw it coming or knew what to do with it. But it was huge.

Everyone had an opinion.

Was it the best thing ever?

Was it the end of music as we knew it?

Again, what the hell were we supposed to do with this?

It wasn't until an interview with 'legendary rap impresario', Dick Clark, of American Bandstand fame, (and a good friend of Redz!), that people finally realized this was a good thing for music, and it was here to stay.

Clark famously said, "anyone that sells almost a million copies of his CD in one week deserves to be listened to."

People shut up, because they knew this was important.

Rap was hip again, and it had something to say.

Yes, Snoop also rapped about 'bitches and money, yo' but he was also a social activist, an equality activist, and, let's be honest—a weed activist.

Preach on, Reverend Snoop, preach on.

People were listening to what he had to say, and they were showing up and paying attention. A lot of new rappers came on the scene trying to do the same things—it was just great.

And thus started the next (and I might argue, last) great wave of rappers that had a message.

That had an important voice.

And they all totally kicked ass.

Snoop Dogg, Eminem, Dre, Biggie, Tupac, Ice Cube, Mobb Deep, Warren G, and the Wu-Tang Clan! I'm sure I'm forgetting some. Who did you like?

But this was a great time for rap. This took it to the next level and made it global. They even made it into the LA *Weekly*! They made every kid pick a side: Tupac or Biggie, East coast or West coast, Bad Boy or Death Row. This was dangerous. People were going to jail and dying over this shit. All of that was tragic, of course, but man—this was just such good music.

Even non-rappers were paying attention. Rap started getting mixed with all other genres, and was now a marketing device to reach people of color at levels we'd never seen before. Rap was back, and it sure as hell wasn't going away.

Chapter 3.2

"Back Stroke Lover Always Hiding 'Neath the Covers"

Rap was huge, but rock wasn't dormant. Rock was finding new ways to express itself as well. Rock started using rap, while rap started using rock. And a whole new mixture of music was born.

Some of it you remember well.

Blondie rapping in "Rapture". I looked it up, and this is considered the first #1 rap song of all time. I love Blondie, she's a legend, an amazing singer, and from what I can tell, a beautiful person, but I'm just not sure I can get on board with this being the first #1 'rap' record. It's a great pop song with some rap thrown in because she took what she heard on the streets of New York and added it to what she already did, but I'm just not sure. What do you think?

The prime example that everybody knows about was

Aerosmith revitalizing its career by teaming up with Run-DMC in their uber-famous remake (and totally kick-ass video) for Walk This Way.

But if you knew where to look, there was so much more. Some of it was amazing, like the duet of Public Enemy and Anthrax doing "Bring the Noise." Some, not so much, like the forced and over-marketed amalgamation of the *Judgment Night* soundtrack. I won't go into detail on this—you can look it up—but I'll sum it up by giving you just one of CD's fancy pairings—Mudhoney and Sir-Mix-a-Lot? Um...

Despite that unfortunate soundtrack, it was obvious that rock or rap no longer had to stay in its own lane. Tone Loc used a hook from Van Halen's "Jamie's Cryin." The Beastie Boys used AC/DC riffs. KISS rapped on "All Hell's Breaking Loose." Even prog-rock legends Rush tried rapping on their hit, "Roll the Bones." That song came out twenty years ago, and I'm still deciding if it's amazing—because I do love me some Rush—or just ridiculous. I have no idea.

All of this eventually gave birth to bands like Limp Bizkit, who recorded some songs with Wu-Tang, KORN, The Kottonmouth Kings, and many others. These bands *started* with the idea of rap and rock together in one song—every song. This was their new genre, and man did the fans love it.

It was an exciting time of experimentation that brought a lot of new fans into the fold of both genres. And it finally made it safe for two scrawny white boys to buy tickets for an Ice Cube concert on Sunset Strip, while making the decision to dress up as cowboys. What could go wrong?

Chapter 3.3

"'Cause You're Getting Fucked Out Your Green, By a White Boy, With No Vaseline"

A guy I worked with, Chris, was about as Southern as you can get. Both the good—he was super polite, very patient, a true gentleman, and as smart as they come. But he also embodied all the stereotypes too—he had a twang in his voice, liked to spit his 'chaw' on the sidewalk while drinking bad American beer, and would pontificate endlessly about why southern music was better than anything.

If I had to hear one more story about why Robert Earl Keen was the best singer ever to come out of Nashville, I swore I was going to poison his Bud Light (But he wasn't wrong, that guy is an amazing singer / songwriter).

Anyway, aside from work, and arguing about music, the one other thing we had in common is that Chris also loved rap. During a slow day at work, I was thumbing through a copy of LA *Weekly* and saw that Ice Cube tickets were going on sale for a concert in a small venue on Sunset Strip. It maybe held four-hundred people. And this was fucking Ice Cube!

Chris and I got tickets the second they went on sale, and we couldn't wait to go.

But we had plans. I'm not saying they were great plans. Looking back, they were probably pretty fucking stupid plans. But we had plans, and we were going to see them through.

On the night of the show, we both dressed in our best blue jeans, lambskin cowboy boots, big 'cowboy' shirts, buckles, and trucker hats—the kind with the annoying mesh on the back.

We looked like we were ready for a Lynyrd Skynyrd concert.

We were ready to drink nothing but Coors Light.

We were kings of the motherfucking Sunset Strip, baby.

And we were going to die.

There aren't too many times in one's life when you play out a scene from a movie. I mentioned *Vertigo* in an earlier chapter. This time it was *Animal House*.

Yes, folks, Chris and I were Boone from the Zeta Beta Tau fraternity screaming, "My Man Otis!

If you don't know the scene, seriously, stop reading this book, and go pick up your well-worn copy of *Pride and Prejudice*, you hoity-toity little shit.

We walked in the venue and it felt like the entire crowd looked right at us.

It felt like Ice Cube himself stopped the show and turned the spotlights on us.

It felt like we were going to get thrown out on our asses.

I was just waiting for someone to come over and say, "do you mind if we dance with yo dates."

"No, we were just leaving!"

But nothing happened.

Rap had changed so much, become so mainstream, had been integrated with all other forms of music, that when the totally mixed-race crowd saw two 'rednecks' enter the venue, they accepted us as just another set of fans, wanting to see a really talented artist and song writer.

And when Cube starting imploring the crowd to yell, "Fuck you, Ice Cube, fuck you, Ice Cube" while he rapped over the top of us, everyone in the crowd, black, white, brown, red, green, and purple, bounced up and down with their fingers in the air, waving like they just don't care, and all was right with the music world!

Chapter 3.4

"Lucid Dreams"

Rap today is all over the place. And, in my opinion, that's not a bad thing. There are tons of songs about "bitches and money, yo." And yes, I still tune those out regularly. But there are great songs about social justice as well, and some seriously great talent.

So maybe I was wrong about Snoop's era being the last great rap era. There's some amazing stuff happening now, and I'm learning it all from my kid!

My son, Tim, has become a rap lover—a huge one, in fact. So much so, that's he wants to go into the booth and cut a track. It's just him and a friend messing around, but he loves the artform so much, that he wants to be a part of it. I love everything about this and wish him nothing but the best, of course. Even if he fails, at least he put his heart and love on the line and gave it a shot. Rock on (Rap on?) Big T, I hope you live your dreams.

But Tim is the one that's shown me the latest and greatest in the rap world for the last ten years or so.

Takashi 6ix9ine, XXX Tentacion, Post Malone, Lil Pump, J Cole, Chance the Rapper, Kendrick Lamar, Juice WRLD, and Lil Skies—who got a face tattoo so he would force himself into pursing his dream knowing that no one would ever hire him again—and so many more.

It's the #1 selling genre of music worldwide on all the Internet sites, so it's not going anywhere. And I'm excited to see what Tim teaches me next.

Junior Varsity Base

When am I supposed to wave my hands in the air....?

all

This changed the world!

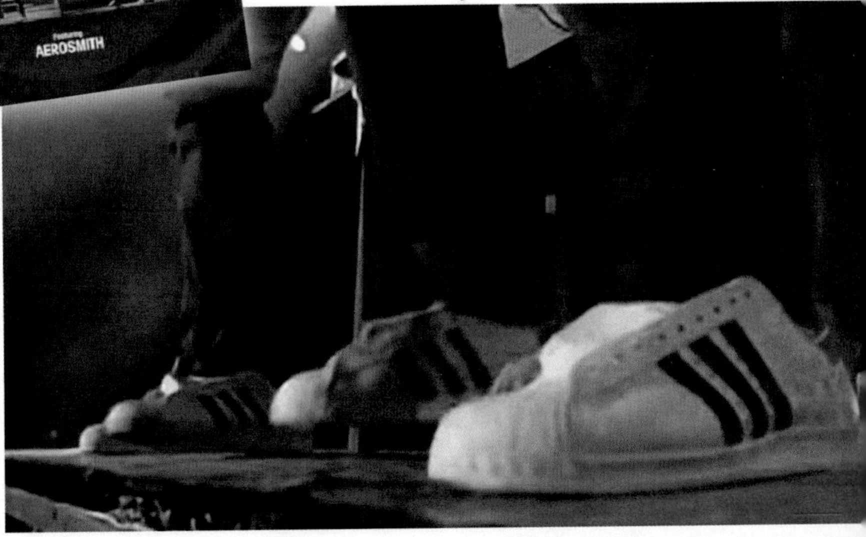

Walk
THIS
Way

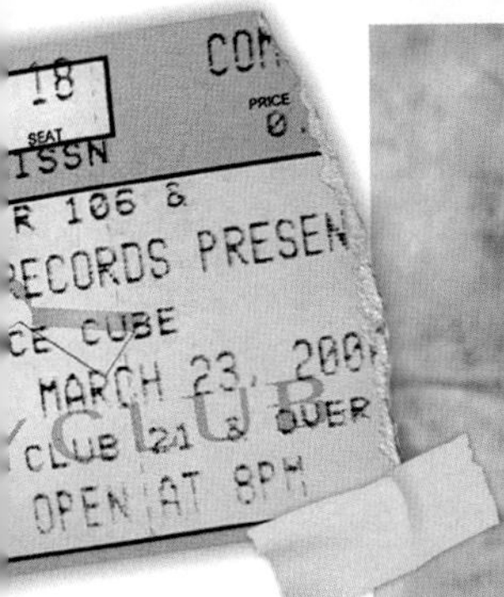

Lucid
Dreams!

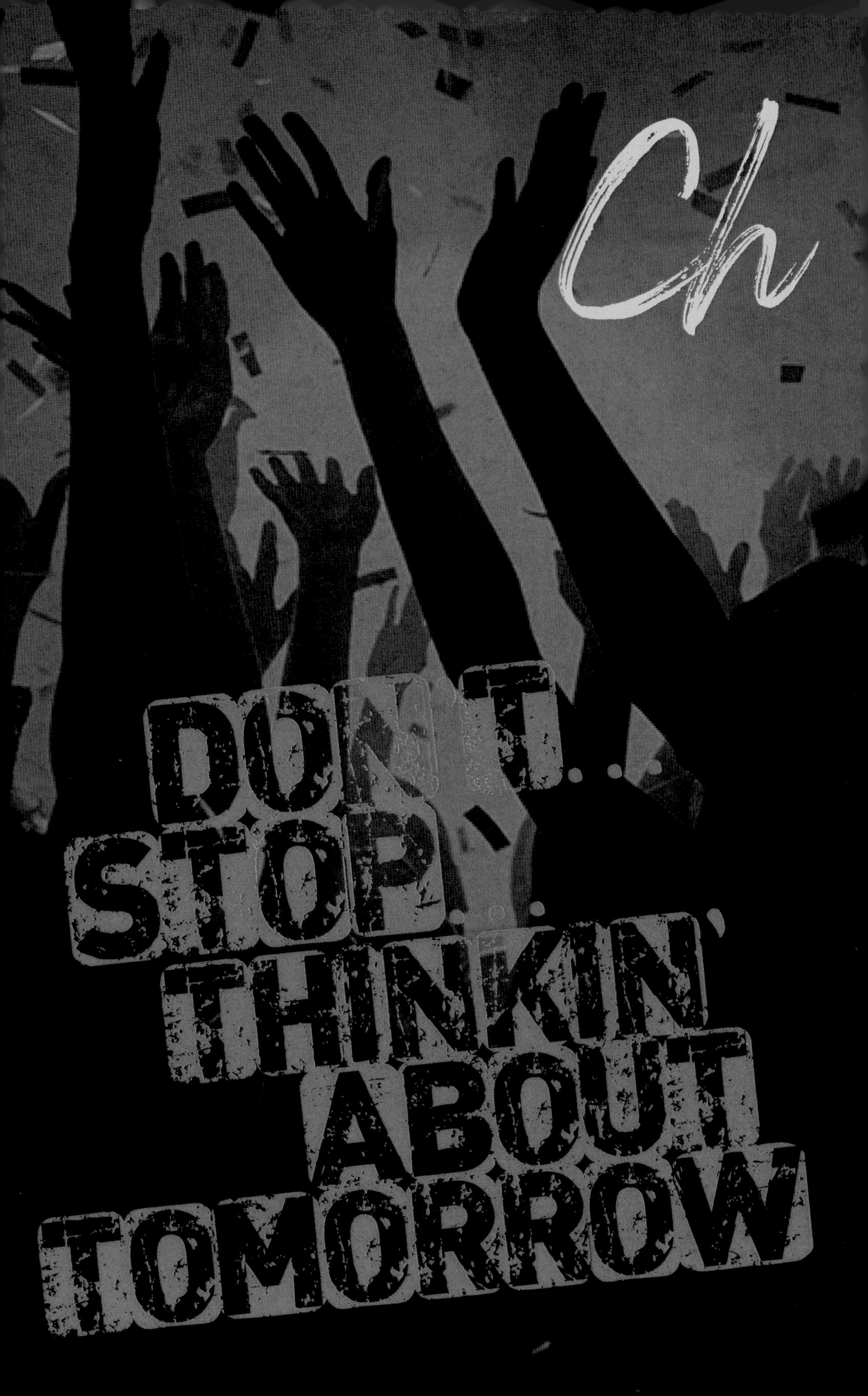
Ch
DON'T...
STOP...
THINKIN'
ABOUT
TOMORROW

apter 4

"Don't...Stop...Thinkin' About Tomorrow"

The West End, and How a Chance Encounter with Mick Fleetwood Turned into the Best Party Years of My Life

Right around college, I discovered something new about music and something new about myself: I could dance!

Dance music certainly wasn't my 'thing,' but when the time came to go out on a Saturday night, you'd be amazed at how fast I could finish that Bon Jovi CD and pop in one by Taylor Dayne.

I was still shy—especially around women. No game whatsoever in that department, although I was certainly a lot better than I was in high school.

I wasn't the best-looking guy in 'my crew.' I certainly didn't have the most money, or best clothes. And I may not have been the funniest... well, maybe... but get me on a dance floor, and watch out. This white boy could sure shake his booty.

My dad used to say it was all his genes, because he had the classic rock, the Philadelphia soul, *and* the Latin dancing in his background. Plus, he played drums and timpani and always kept a good beat.

My mom would say the same thing, claiming it was her Motown upbringing, her hippie ways in the '60s, or all those times she spent in discos and clubs—where she eventually met my dad.

I was happy to take both, thank you very much.

But it wasn't always this way.

Back at the end of high school, all my friends wanted to go to all the happening 18-and-over clubs in Hollywood and LA, with the biggest and best being The Florentine Gardens.

This thing was literally a warehouse-sized party spot in some seedy part of L.A. where people lined up for hours before opening to get in and lined up for hours after at the taco trucks that knew we needed to eat before we all went home.

I even got not one, but two, fake IDs, so I could get into places like The Florentine Gardens at age 17.

The first ID was hilarious. I drove to someone's house in Venice, CA, and in his basement, his entire wall was painted to look like an Idaho Driver's License. All ten feet of it! You would stand in front of it, so your head 'fit' in the photo area, he would take the picture, print it out, laminate it, and send you on your way—for thirty-five dollars, of course.

I often wonder how many seventeen-year old kids in L.A. that year lived at that same address in Boise!

Needless to say, that one didn't last very long. I got into a few clubs, but one surly bouncer took an extra-long look at my ID one day, said 'hell no,' threw it in the trash, and kicked me out of the line. I went home. Didn't even get tacos that night, dammit.

After that, I upped my game. A buddy of mine (who shall remain nameless) had a friend (who shall also remain nameless) who worked at a hospital and could get real California issued birth certificates, for a hefty price, which I think was around a hundred dollars. For a seventeen-year-old kid, that was a ton of cash.

Anyway, I purchased one of those birth certificates, dressed up in the best clothes I had in my closet, and headed on down to the Santa Monica DMV to get a real California ID card. The driver's license would have involved an extra test, so I just went with the ID card, knowing that it would have all the seals, all the security tags, and all the reality of a state-issued ID card.

This is also where I had my first true gay experience as well.

Now, hold on, it's not what you think.

I have absolutely zero issue with anyone loving anyone else and I wish you all the happiness in the world no matter who you are. I just wasn't prepared for it myself, at the DMV, while trying to get my 'fake' real ID.

I stood in line in my dapper clothes, which really was just khakis and a button-down. Normally, I was into wearing board shorts, tank tops, and Vans so this was not my usual look.

I finally got to the front of the line, a bit nervous, slightly sweaty, but trying to be confident in pulling off my ID caper.

I handed my paperwork to the handsome young gentlemen behind the counter, including my 'birth certificate' complete with fake name, a friend's address, and a ton of new information about me that I spent weeks memorizing.

He looked at the paperwork.

He looked at me.

He looked back at the paperwork.

He looked back at me.

He leaned over the counter, looked me up and down, and said, "Well, I'm not sure these documents are legit, but... (paused again as he looked me up and down... again) ...but I'll do it just for you!"

He gave me a smile, and a wink, and went back to what he was doing.

Feeling a little awkward–I mean, at this point in my life, I had very few instances of *girls* hitting on me, and now I just had my first guy hitting on me–and trying to suppress the lump in my throat, I instantly seized on the opportunity and said "thank you" with the best smile I could conjure up.

I was going to get that ID and get my dancing-ass into those clubs if it was the last thing I do!

He stamped the paperwork and sent me on my way.

The real California ID arrived at my friend's place about four-to-five weeks later, and I snatched it up, after having to buy him lunch of course—so he wouldn't narc on me.

But this got me in. I could get into The Florentine Gardens and all the other under 21 clubs. I could go dance.

The music was insane, and the dance moves were legendary. To this day, I would kick each and every one of your butts on the dance floor if we had a contest to do the Running Man, or the Cabbage Patch, or any number of other dances that had names like that back in the day.

Do dances still have names? I haven't kept up with that. But these were the two hot ones of the day, and I knew them well.

I would watch the crowds, trying to follow what they were doing, and to what songs. I would totally steal their moves, and wouldn't care one single bit what anyone thought.

And maybe, just maybe, on a night I was feeling confident, I would ask a girl to dance. It didn't happen often, and when it did, nine times out of ten, they'd say no. But when it worked, it was great. It made me feel like dance music was making my life a bit better, and I loved every second of it.

So, by the time I got to college, I was pretty darn good.

I was in a fraternity for a while—about three semesters—but I got kicked out for not paying my dues. I ate ramen and peanut butter and jelly most days in college, so no way could I keep up with those dues. Still the biggest mistake Lambda Chi Alpha ever made if you ask me.

But for those three semesters, we had parties almost every weekend. Dance parties with girls, and no cover charge! And it was a lot of fun to show off my new L.A.-Club-dance-moves. And the girls actually wanted to dance with me! Okay, the cheap beer probably helped, but give me a little credit, would ya? My confidence soared. A different kind of music filled up my dance card, as well as my dating card quite a bit during those three semesters. Maybe I'll save those stories for another book.

Chapter 4.1

"*Try A Little Tenderness*"

Did you like the movie *The Commitments*?

Seriously, if you didn't, why on earth are you reading this book?

The image of that white, Irish saxophone player sitting on a rock, pretending he's James Brown, and saying "I'm blick, and imma proud" is just so hilarious.

If you haven't seen it, it's probably a bit dated by now, but it's still just so well written and so well acted. I highly recommend.

Well, in the early- to mid-'90s, Commitment-like tribute bands were all the rage, and the best one in L.A. was at The West End, in Santa Monica.

The West End was a small box of a club located on the corner of 5th and Arizona in the heart of the beachside city I grew up in. It really wasn't that much to look at, but it had that family-run dive bar quality that most of us would love to drink at, I assume.

In fact, The West End *was* family run, and I never would have gone there, if it wasn't for Mick Fleetwood.

I was chatting one day with an assistant at A&M Records, when I worked there as an intern. We were talking about all kinds of music, what we liked, the power of live shows (which we'll dive into in a future chapter), and all sorts of other music-related topics. To be honest, it just made the time fly by while I was stuffing Del Amitri CD's to send to radio stations all over the United States. Great CD, by the way.

She casually mentioned to me that her aunt owned a club in Santa Monica, right near where I lived, called The West End, and that Mick Fleetwood was playing there that weekend as a guest drummer for some local band. Would I want to go? She could get my name at the door, plus one.

I told you, assistants are the best people to know!

With a resounding yes, my roommate and I headed off to the show. The legendary Mick Fleetwood walks to the kit, does a bunch of great local rock and blues numbers with his buddy on stage, stays behind to shake a few hands, and then goes about his day as if sitting and playing rock standards on a drum kit is something he does every day. Oh wait...

We got to shake his hand and tell him we were fans, all the usual stuff. He was so laid back and cool and just wanted everyone to appreciate his buddy on stage and wanted us to buy *their* CD, and so on. He was truly a giving individual, and I'm lucky to have been one of the hundred or so fans in attendance that evening.

But a cool thing happened after that as well.

We hung out with the owner—my friend's aunt. She bought us drinks, so we loved her right away, naturally. But she told us to come back that Friday and Saturday and check out the club in its true form. Packed to the gills with sweaty young adults, dancing their butts off to the sounds of a Commitments-like tribute band on Friday, and an '80s cover band, called The Legwarmers, on Saturday.

We were intrigued.

We gathered a few friends and arrived about an hour after the club opened on a Friday night. We could never be on time, right? That's such an un-club, un-L.A. thing to do. Club etiquette dictated that you never wanted to be the first one there.

Oops.

The place was already packed, and there was a growing line outside the door.

Now, as you now, there are a few tactics clubs use to attract new patrons. For example, some clubs will purposely keep people outside the door, even when the inside is only half-full, just to show all the people driving by that this place is so "hip and happening" that you need to stop here too!

But this wasn't that; this place was packed. And if we didn't get in line soon, we weren't getting in for the evening.

Luckily the Commitments band played a few sets, and after the first set ended, dozens of people left and went to the next happening spot, I suppose.

We got in and found the aunt to say hello and hopefully get some more free drinks, which she happily obliged us—while doing a shot of tequila herself. Damn, don't you just love bar owners?

The place was filling up again—with quite a few lovely young ladies, I might add. Apparently, they all loved the Commitments movie too! This was going to be great.

The eight or nine-piece band came on stage for their second set, and totally fooled the crowd. The started off with "Try a Little Tenderness" by the incomparable Otis Redding. Not many people knew what was coming, but I wasn't one of them. You could tell the crowd was a bit befuddled by the slow jam playing before them.

"Oh, she may be weary
Them young girls they do get wearied
Wearing that same old shaggy dress, yeah, yeah"

As you know that song builds and builds until you reach the crashing crescendo with the horn section and backup singers, and soulful Otis singing his very best.

By the end of that song, the crowd was a mess. They were cheering, jumping, dancing, screaming, and whopping it up—begging for more.

I think the band did the entire Commitments movie soundtrack that set, plus a ton of other standards, including my personal favorite, "Vehicle", by The Ides of March. Google this song right now if you don't know it.

Pretty good, right?

After about two hours of this, and numerous cocktails, we headed home to sleep off our evening, and get ready for the next one.

We headed back Saturday night to check out the other cool band we were told about, The Legwarmers.

I found out much later in life that many cities across the country had an '80s cover band called The Legwarmers. Apparently, this is *the* 80's cover band name. I've seen the one in D.C., where I currently live, more than a few times—and they are no better, no worse, than the one I saw at The West End all those years ago. That same band in D.C. also plays in a '90s cover band too, dubbed White Ford Bronco, which is literally the most perfect 90's band name ever. Right, OJ?

Anyway, Saturday night was filled with all the same fun and excitement (and shots) as we had on Saturday, but the vibe was much more of a party atmosphere. People my age reliving their '80s glory years while grinding on someone they just met, to "Eye of the Tiger," or "Oh, Mickey, You're So Fine," or "Don't You Want Me, Baby."

As my dancing skills got me noticed on the dance floor, I felt my confidence growing too, and would start asking as many girls to dance as possible. Many said yes, and many said no—but I no longer cared.

The music changed me.

I was no longer the wallflower I used to be. No longer afraid to say excruciatingly weird stuff to a girl, like "hello, how are you?" No longer worried about what would happen to me if they said no.

I'm not sure I was still any good at this outside-the-club scene, but at least this was very good practice, and I sure practiced a lot.

In fact, you might say I got my first taste at being a bit cocky during this time.

You don't wanna dance with me? Me? Okay, fine, I'm gonna

get you out on the dance floor anyway because yeah, I can do that now. Watch these moves, baby!

Well, that didn't endear me to many of the ladies in the club on a given night, but it's worth noting I had gone from totally shy to a total asshole, in the amount of time it took to dance to Billie Jean.

Regardless, my buddies and I spent, almost literally, every Friday and Saturday night at The West End for the next two years.

That was our spot.

You want to go? We can get you in!

You want free drinks? We know the bartenders!

Cover charge? No friend of Ken pays a cover charge.

We like to think we ruled that place, we owned it, and no one could take it from us—but all good things come to an end. After about two years, the crew split apart, went their separate ways, and only gathered at The West End occasionally from that point forward to talk about all the good times we used to have there.

So, what happened to The West End, you ask?

I just looked it up while writing this, and I'm sad to say, but The West End is no more. It was bought out by some investment group and they turned it into a club called Canary, complete with ferns and flowers flowing out of the walls (ferns, really?), overpriced drinks, and a "more refined nightlife experience" according to their website. If that's your thing, great, but I promise you'll never have as much fun as we did in the days of The Commitments and The Legwarmers.

Go enjoy your apple martini!

Chapter 4.2

"Devil with a Blue Dress On"

A quick story—perhaps a caution—about taking my newfound confidence a bit too far.

My first 'real' job, where I wasn't waiting tables, was at Columbia Home Entertainment—part of the Sony Pictures empire, in Culver City, CA.

I was a lowly assistant, and then a coordinator, but that's okay. It was exactly what first jobs were supposed to be like. I shuffled papers all day, sent out packages to our offices overseas, and otherwise dealt with whatever the boss told me to deal with. They were cool, and I had no complaints.

It wasn't music, for reasons we'll discuss shortly, but it was still entertainment close to home, which suited me just fine.

Plus, instead of getting free music, I got free DVD's—which was this brand-new movie delivery mechanism that was taking off across the globe.

And instead of running into Soundgarden, like when I ran across the A&M lot, when I ran across the Sony lot, I ran into famous actors, like the time I, once again, *literally* ran into LL Cool J. Super nice guy. Super big dude. Super big muscles. Super happy to apologize and get out of there as fast as possible. Maybe I should start looking where I'm going, eh?

Anyway, Sony had all these offices and affiliates around the world. An office in France, an affiliate office in Prague, and they were all set up to help us sell our DVD's in those countries, or throughout Europe, Asia, and wherever. It was a vast network set up to push products out to the masses. Movies like *Charlie's Angels*, *Men in Black*, *Gladiator*, or the world-famous *Trumpet of the Swan* (animated version). Hey, it's a classic, ok?

One year, Sony called all the international offices into L.A. for a week long meeting about how to make *Trumpet of the Swan* the biggest selling DVD in movie history, the best ways to market *Trumpet of the Swan*, the right images to use, the right stores to sell to, and on and on. Okay, it wasn't just that movie, but you get the point.

At the end of that week-long heavily-intensive pro-Trumpet-of-the-Swan-(animated)-DVD meeting, Sony decided we're going to have a party, and a talent show, pitting one office against the other for the right to call themselves the most talented Sony DVD sales office on Planet Earth, and the home office was taking volunteers to be a part of this amazing opportunity.

I was not the least bit interested.

But all my colleagues were doing it.

There were planning meetings. There were song ideas. There were rehearsals. There was a lot of fun going on, and I was conspicuously absent from it.

Finally, after almost every other colleague in my department signed up, the burden became too great, and I signed up to be part of the team. Fuck you, peer pressure.

Our plan was to all get on stage and dance and sing to the Will Smith song, "Men in Black". The fun light little rap ditty he put out when the first movie first came out.

"Here come the Men in Black

They won't let you remember..."

Yeah, that one.

But there was a catch.

As part of our entry into this event, each member of the team was 'required' to head down to the Sony Pictures Costume Department and wear a costume from another Sony movie. Any Sony movie.

And this was the *actual* Costume Department that all actors went to before they went on set and did their movies! This was no joke.

I reluctantly went down to that area and chatted with the person in charge at the time.

"Oh, you're another one of those Men in Black dancers, aren't you," she said while trying as hard as humanly possible not to roll her eyes at me. She had thirty six-feet-tall men to fit with Planet of the Apes costumes that week, she couldn't be seen spending more than a few seconds helping me.

"Can I have one of the ape costumes," I asked?

She turned to me and gave me her well-worn speech.

"You're not getting anything new, you're getting old movies, costumes that no one will need again on set. We *are* a working functional studio, you know."

Ah, L.A., home of the calm and easy-going people.

"Ok, well what do you have for me?" I asked.

She went in back and came out with the costume worn by Joaquin Phoenix in *Gladiator*!

Holy shit!

I was going to be Commodus, the twisted son of Marcus Aurelius! The guy who fought Russell Crowe in the arena. I could definitely get behind that!

I just couldn't get into it.

Joaquin Phoenix had to be 3 feet tall.

Ok, I looked it up, he's 5'8". But I'm 6'2". This wasn't going to work.

"What else you got?" I asked.

"The only thing I have in your size is that," she said, while pointing at a bridesmaid's dress.

A bridesmaid's dress worn in the Julia Roberts movie *My Best Friend's Wedding*. It wasn't Julia's. It was some other actor, probably an extra, from one of the wedding scenes, but I didn't care.

I thought about it for a second, and feeling a swell of cocky confidence I learned to have from the dance floor at The West End, I said, "sure, I'll take it, why not. I'll own this dress!"

"Whatever," said the costume lady while walking away,

"Just bring it back in one piece."

I brought the dress back to my cubicle, fully confident I could pull this off. I attended the rehearsals, learned the dance movies, and memorized that damn song top to bottom.

We were gonna crush this competition!

Yeah, ummm...

We sucked.

We couldn't carry a collective tune, were all over the place on our dance steps, and were so totally out of sync that members of the team just started doing their own thing. I remembered my boss, dressed in a full *Stuart Little* outfit, went into the crowd and started high-fiving people. Others started dancing some disco moves, or the Running Man, or the Watusi for all I know.

I followed suit and did the worm.

Yup.

You read that correctly.

Wearing a light blue backless bridesmaid dress, I got down on the ground in front of the stage and did the fucking worm for a hundred or so of my closest Sony colleagues from around the world.

Yeah. Think about that for a second.

So professional.

So demure (But don't worry, I had bicycle shorts on underneath!).

So utterly sad.

The lesson here: perhaps I might have been better off staying a little humble. Perhaps I took my newfound confidence a bit too far, thinking I could pull this off. Perhaps I should have thought better about this particular outfit or signed up a little earlier to get a better costume!

Perhaps, being a fan of music, that led me to this fateful decision, wasn't always a good thing?

That couldn't be it, could it?

Anyone wanna do the Running Man....?

My dance getaway for 2 years

SONY PICTURES ENTERTAINMENT
Deee-Lite
groove is in the heart!!!
music factory
YOUNG MC
Bust it!
BUST·A·MOVE
I looked damn good in that dress!
CHARLIE'S ANGELS

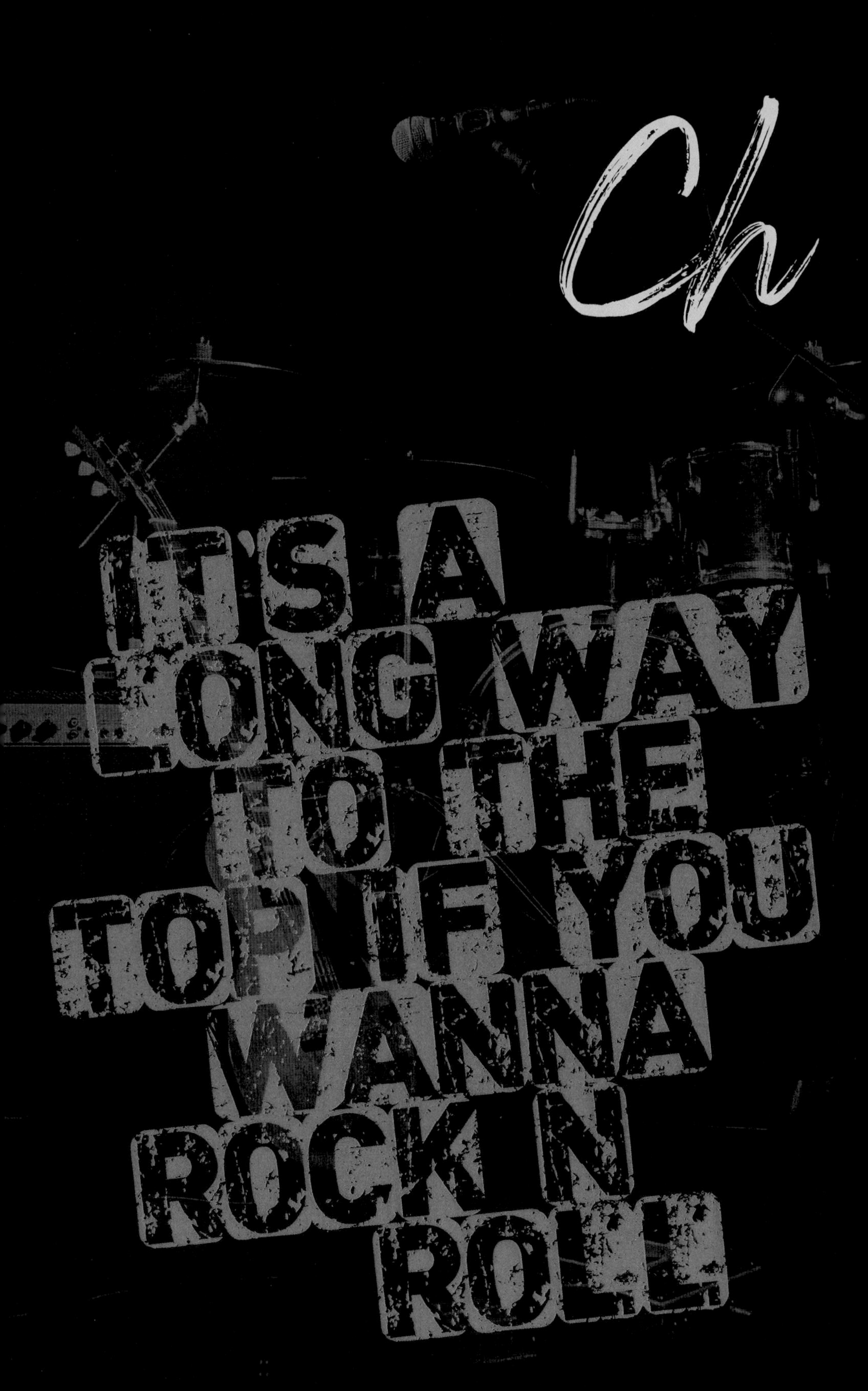
Ch
IT'S A LONG WAY TO THE TOP IF YOU WANNA ROCK N ROLL

apter 5

"It's a Long Way to the Top if You Wanna Rock n Roll"

So Why the Fuck Aren't YOU in a Band, you Name-Dropping POS?

So, by this time, I'm sure a lot of you are saying:

"Hey Ken... what the hell is wrong with you? You were surrounded by music, you worked in the industry, your dad knew everyone, why the hell didn't you learn an instrument, start a band, and get out on the road, you lazy-ass slacker?"

Fair question.

The truth is, I tried.

I tried just about everything a young music lover could try!

When I was seven or eight years old, my parents urged me to take piano lessons. I flatly refused, and since I was the only child, I naturally got my way. I kind of wished they didn't give in on this point, because I would have received some great early music education.

Then fast forward fifteen years, and with all that great piano knowledge, I could have been the piano player for Guns N Roses Use Your Illusion 1 and 2 instead of that Dizzy Reed fellow. What did he have that I didn't?

I would have crushed my parts on November Rain.

So yeah, I should have started young, but much rather preferred to play with my toys and comic books and baseball cards and not go actually learn something from Ms. Crabapple the piano teacher down the street. My bad.

That's part of the reason I was so excited to work at A&M records. I thought "wow, this is it, my big break." I can finally do what I should have done with those piano lessons, make something out of myself in the music world. So, like I said, I learned, listened, and watched everything I could in the year that I was there. I did all the menial chores, volunteered to help where I could, and stayed late to stuff more envelopes to more radio stations on more than one occasion. All in the hopes they would hire me after the internship was over.

They didn't. And there were two reasons for that.

One was on me, the other was because the record industry was about to undergo a huge change, and I'm not sure any music fan, or music company employee saw it coming.

I'm not actually talking about the digital revolution, from Napster to iTunes, although that certainly played into the equation long after I worked in the business.

I'm talking about consolidation.

A&M Records was bought by PolyGram, out of the UK, in 1989, and almost immediately, PolyGram, was looking for a way to move their new assets around to other companies, which they finally did, to Seagram's. Yes, the drink manufacturer that brought you Crown Royal, of all places, in 1998.

Years later, Seagram's, through the Universal Music Group, merged A&M with Geffen and Interscope Records. Today, A&M doesn't really exist as a label, but its catalog was managed by Verve Records, and Interscope—as both were part of the Universal Empire.

All this consolidation led to labels all around the industry consuming other labels all around the industry. And as usually happens, the pool of available jobs was getting a lot smaller.

But I was the intern extraordinaire, wasn't I? They saw me stuffing those packages, attending those meetings, running all sorts of shit across the lot whenever they snapped their fingers, and doing any and all other menial tasks they assigned me to do? Surely, I was a shoo-in for some sort of low-level just-out-of-college type job that nobody wanted, right?

Well, right about then was when I got my first taste of ego in the entertainment industry. And it hit me like a ton of bricks.

I will say upfront, this was mostly my fault—but man, it still stung.

One of the great things about working in this environment was all the bullshit. I don't mean the stress and stupid orders from the VP and stuff like that. I mean the camaraderie. The back and forth. The needling each other. The jokes. The water cooler chit-chat. You know, the bullshit.

I was in one of these situations one day with a colleague. He was throwing some great B.S. my way—about being a red head, about going to a 'lame school' like Cal State Northridge, about my taste in music, about anything he could find. And I was giving as good as I was getting. It was a fun time. People were laughing at me, at him, and at us. All good, and no worries.

It reminded me of that scene in Goodfellas where Joe Pesci, Ray Liotta, Robert DeNiro and others are playing poker in the basement, and Spider, played by the amazing Michael Imperioli, has to bring them drinks. They're teasing Spider incessantly. The beginning of that is great and that's exactly what it felt like.

Unfortunately, it also felt like the end of that scene too. Spider eventually tells Pesci to go fuck himself and the table goes nuts. So, Pesci takes out his gun and shoots him 5,713 times, or so it seems, and then goes back to the card game. Fucking brilliant. I love that movie.

Anyway, so I'm going back and forth with this guy, giving as good as I'm getting, and I make a fatal mistake. I made a joke about his receding hairline.

Oops.

Apparently, that was a bridge too far.

He pulled out his gun and, in front of everyone, shot me 5,713 times and I died, and then got a role on the Sopranos as Tony's bitch.

Well, okay, not really, but it felt like it.

Because the next day I was in the office, I got called into the hiring manager, and was told that there were no longer any positions available for me.

Poof.

Over.

No more record company.

No more dream of signing bands.

I took a swing, landed a blow, and got disqualified from the fight. Down for the count.

After a year at A&M working my ass off, for no money, the ride ended, and I went home.

Shit.

Huge lesson learned in that moment. It's okay to bullshit with people above you, but always treat them with respect, even if you must take a few extra hits to do so. Or you end up like Spider.

One irony of that moment is that, as I'm sitting here writing this, my hair is half gone. Fucking karma!

I went back to the drawing board, looking for work anywhere in the entertainment industry, which in L.A., is just about everywhere. I was still waiting tables, and earning some money, so it's not like that little incident put me out on the street, but I had to scramble after what I thought was a sure thing, and it took a few months to get back on my feet.

I ended up at MGM Studios, and then Sony, where I ended up in that blue dress. So, everything worked out in the end. And I looked damn good in that dress.

To be perfectly fair to A&M, they did offer me a job a little while later. I could have been a production assistant in the booth where the artists are recording the songs. That would have been amazing.

Um, excuse me, Mr. Springsteen, but your vocals just weren't right on that cut, can we try it again please. And a one and a two…

Super cool, right? But they offered me the 1am to 7am shift, and, to be honest, the money was almost worse than what I "earned" as an unpaid intern!

I would have had to give up waiting tables, and grad school would have been impossible, so I thanked them and turned it down. Another opportunity lost? Maybe. Tough to say.

I was happy at MGM and Sony while I was working on getting my MBA. And frankly, I wanted to sleep at night. But I kept hustling in music. This time, working for bands I was just "sure" were going to be the next big thing.

Chapter 5.1

"Roll Down the Window as I Pull Out of the Driveway"

We've all been there. We've all had those moments. We've all seen those shows. We all have those friends, right?

"Dude, Ken, I'm in this new band, and we play Mexican Jazz Fusion Polka, with a twist of Slayer, and you gotta come see us, and the cover is only five bucks, and a ton of chicks will be there, and it's gonna be rad."

So we go, and pay we the cover, and we look at the girls, and we maybe talk to some, although maybe not, because we still sorta suck at doing that, and we buy the overpriced eight-dollar Corona Light, because it's the cheapest beer they have, and we get up to the front of the stage and we throw our metal horns in the air.

And man, do they suck.

Somewhere between their mash-up of "Raining Blood" with "La Bamba", and "Dead Skin Mask" and The Weird Al version of

"Feliz Navidad" on accordion, you find a reason—any goddam reason—to put the beer down, curse the fact that you just wasted eight dollars, and slip out the side door while running to your car, hoping you can make it home to catch the last half hour of Saturday Night Live.

Now of course, the next day you see your friend at Jamba Juice, you tell him how much his whole show fucking rocked, and does he have a CD, and that you promise you'll get it out to all the friends you still have at A&M Records and we'll see what happens. So, it all ends on a positive note!

I tried my hand at working for a couple of bands that I was certain were going to make it.

Like bigger than Nirvana! Bigger than Michael Jackson! Bigger than The Spice Girls!

That's where my head was, at least. But I loved music, and I loved their music—so I went to work for them—for free, again—with all my heart and soul.

Bands that haven't made it yet are just the best. They're like Avis—the car rental company. Their slogan is "We Try Harder." Well, local bands just try harder. They'll do anything. They'll play anywhere. They'll befriend anyone. And usually they are super sincere to boot.

The first band I worked for was a cool local LA/Santa Barbara band called Munkafust.

Ok, I know, not the best name, and you're probably saying, 'uh yeah, no wonder they didn't get big.' I think the name came from some drunken soiree the band members had at some point in their past.

"Let's call our band Pink Elephant Bong Load, dude."

"How about something really stupid like Ned's Atomic Dustbin!" (Sorry, Ned, just teasing.)

"I got it! How about Munkafust!"

Winner!

Or something like that I'm sure.

Epic.

But the music... that shit was good!

Solid Rock n Roll core. Great vocals. Excellent musicians. Just a good fucking band. The kind of band I would actually finish my overpriced Corona Light so I could stay for the whole set and give them a high-five after the gig, sparing myself any further embarrassing moments at Jamba Juice!

They had a song called "Beaten to the Ground" which was like a welcome kick to the head with a forty-year-old combat boot. That thing fucking rocked. Go find it if you can.

So, because of that song, and because of that band, and how cool the guys were, and because I knew the manager, I went to work for them for one summer back in the mid-90s.

This time, I didn't stuff envelopes. I was their promotions man, their tour manager, their press guy, their 'go-fer' and ok, their envelope stuffer. But this shit was gonna look good on my Rock n Roll resume when I went for my next real job.

I sent CD's to record labels. I called college radio, urging them to play it. I even set up a midwestern summer tour for the band. Complete with stops in more than twenty cities, travel arrangements, hotel rooms, and the whole nine yards. Shit, that was a lot of work, man!

And I went to every local gig I could. I put up posters and flyers on every light pole in a twenty-mile radius. I got all my friends, and all their friends to go. I got people who worked behind the counter at Jamba Juice to go. I was everywhere.

Along with their official manager, we ran the whole gig for three-to-four months, and, not for nothing–it was a pretty good year for them, at least in my humble opinion.

When summer was over, I went back to grad school, and they continued on with their touring, their recording, and their rocking. I lost track of them over the years. They still play around L.A. from what I can tell. Apparently, Trip, in Santa Monica, is still a place you can see them. Go check them out if you can. I promise it'll be a damn good time. And Trip is pretty cool too!

The next band I worked for–for no money (by now, you

think I'd learn!)—were some close friends I still have to this day. They must have really appreciated all my free work to put up with me for this long.

I met Jess at The Cheesecake Factory, Woodland Hills, in the mid-90s. He was everybody's favorite server. Great attitude. Great teacher. Looked great in those ridiculous white jeans they forced us to wear. And he had great long Rock n Roll hair. Like Tom Cruise in Top Gun type hair—only longer. Just perfect.

We became buds right away, as soon as he said, "dude, you gotta come see my band!"

And no, it wasn't Mexican Polka mixed with Slayer. Although, like you, I have literally been thinking about what a mash-up of *Raining Blood* and *La Bamba* might actually sound like since I wrote that half a chapter ago. Yo, Internet, get on that, would ya?

"The sky is turning red
Para bailar la bamba
Return to power draws near
Se necisita una poca de gracia"

Shit, this could work!

Anyway, Jess was in a band called Pincushion Jones. They fucking rocked. More than that. They were a really good band that was going places. And I was going to be their roadie.

And because I was their roadie, they were going to give me something I have always wanted—my very own bonafide kick-ass cool Rock n Roll nickname. Like Meatloaf, or The Toxic Twins, or Axl, or Slash, or Sting, or Snoop, or even the motherfucking Captain and Tennille!

And I got one!

Twenty-five years later.

Bastards.

Let me explain.

The first time I saw Pincushion Jones play was at the world-famous Toby Jug—a bar the size of your living room in a shitty part of "the 818", or what you know as "The Valley" in Los Angeles. I think it was surrounded by two or three auto mechanics at the time. And for the last twenty years, it has been a different club, still trying to break the next big valley band.

But back then, it was perfect—for a couple of reasons.

One, I got to see my buds perform for the first time at a very unintimidating place. And two, the night they played was free pizza night. Fucking score!

"Great song guys, um, can you pass the pepperoni, please."

Perfect.

Jess, Dave, Scott, and Leigh had just finished making their latest album, *Violent Mood Swings*, and they were gonna perform those songs that night at the Toby Jug. Sort of an 818-style record release party, if you will, with pizza.

They tore it up that night.

Classic Rock n Roll with some cool metal as well as some great acoustic stuff. And a couple of really bad songs too, like the song "Me", which said the word "me" like five-hundred times. Oof. But hey, not every song could be "Hotel California."

They even did a metal cover of Pink Floyd's "Hey You" which had the whole crowd banging their head. Listening to Dave, the lead singer, scream "and the worms ate into his brrrrrrrrraaaaaaaaiiiiiiiiinnnsssss...." is not something you easily forget.

I started working with these guys right then and there. I brought them their guitars from the side of the stage. I got them pitchers of Meister-Brau beer for the Happy Hour price of $3.50, and I even helped sell their CD to their new adoring fans. Alas, I never did see my cut from those sales.

But I didn't want money. All I wanted was some music experience, and a cool nickname. Something I could put on a t-shirt. Something that screamed 'that dude is with the band."

It was a small ask, right? Jess was known as "Shorty" because, well, the man just wasn't very tall. Dave liked to call himself "Diamond Dave"—but that was already taken by some guy with blonde hair in some band you may have heard of, so most people just called him "Meat," as in "Why does he keep calling me Meat," from Bull Durham. Even their manager Dan had the amazing nickname of "Big Sexy." Why couldn't I be "Big Sexy"? Or "Red Sexy"? Or something totally amazing like that. Something that would get me all the girls throwing themselves at Pincushion Jones. Or, at least the ones they didn't want to deal with. That would be okay with me!

So, after the gig, I asked them if I could have one.

"Hey, call me Rojo, I like that nickname!"

In unison, they all told me to fuck off. How DARE I ask for a nickname. A nickname is earned. It isn't given. You don't request one. What the ever-loving fuck was wrong with you? Oh, and please pass me a slice of sausage pizza.

Well, shit.

So, I didn't have my nickname, but I still had my undying love for their music. So, I went to work.

Like Munkafust, I was gonna make a big deal out of these guys. I was gonna put up posters, and get people to the next show, and tell everyone at The Cheesecake Factory they had to be there. They were gonna be huge.

They played everywhere they could find—Bourbon Square, Mancini's, FM Station, Jeremiah's Steak House, after the dinner rush cleared out of course, even the Pelican's Retreat.

Pelican's Retreat was a fun place. Sort of half-Valley, half-beach bar, it was an odd mixture of surfers, valley dudes, chicks with big '80s hair, and angry motorcycle-gang-like lesbians that could kick my ass. But the place was huge, the drinks were cheap, and Pincushion Jones was on the stage!

Pincushion Jones was getting noticed. No, not because of the Toby Jug. But because songs like "The Driveway" were so amazingly good. People were noticing, and random fans would show up. The word was getting out. It was their time, and it was a lot of fun.

They even got to play the Roxy on Sunset Strip. Yes, I know many bands can do that with a simple phone call, but this was big for them. There were people in the crowd. This was happening!

The set that night was electric. They owned that crowd. Every scream, and every note was just on point.

Leigh, the bassist, even came out into the crowd during one song for some impromptu bass solo during one of their songs, which had the crowd going wild, and the boys on stage cracking up. They didn't take themselves too seriously; there was no major ego, and that was good to see. That was a selling point.

It was all we talked about for weeks. What a great gig.

I think the next gig after that was at Bourbon Square, and frankly, it was kind of a letdown. You don't play The Staples Center and then play your friend's backyard BBQ and expect the same vibe. That's what it felt like.

But, like I said, there were people in the crowd. They were getting noticed. And people were making some pretty big decisions.

Sadly, those decisions didn't go in their favor.

I found out some time after the Roxy gig that that show was a big reason they almost got signed, ironically, to A&M Records. According to "Meat", A&M had room to sign one band, and it was down to Pincushion Jones, or this obscure sounding band from Santa Barbara called Dishwalla (Did every band come from Santa Barbara??).

Both were tearing up the L.A. scene. Both had charismatic lead singers, great musicians, solid drummers, catchy songs, good hooks, and radio 'playability.'

But there could be only one.

Well, as you know, A&M went with Dishwalla, who put out their debut album, *Pet Your Friends*, in 1996, and blew up the radio with their hit, "Counting Blue Cars". A great song, and a great album, I must admit, but it meant that Pincushion Jones had missed their big break at that moment.

They played together for a bit longer after the Roxy and

Bourbon Square shows, but then broke up to form other bands and find or continue in their real jobs. Jess went on to play in DAYSIX and started an Internet company. Dave formed GOCR—or Gods of Cock Rock—which, c'mon, is one of the best band names of all time. But guess how much radio airplay that band would ever get? He also worked as a financial analyst. Not sure where Scott and Leigh ended up, but they were solid musicians and super great guys so I'm sure they landed somewhere.

Twenty-five years later, Jess and Dave now play in a great Tom Petty tribute band called Heartbreak Over Petty, formed after Tom passed away on October 2, 2017. They were huge fans of this classic American songwriter and legendary singer. So they formed a band in his honor for one or two gigs around Los Angeles.

And boom.

People just fucking loved it.

Everyone loved Tom Petty, right?

So, those two planned gigs have now turned into three or four years of playing in this band.

You can see them all over L.A., including, ironically, at that same Trip place in Santa Monica. Except for that one Roxy show, I don't think I've ever seen them perform for larger crowds. They put on a good show. You knew all the lyrics. Everyone danced. And it's a goddam good Rock n Roll time.

And thanks to Heartbreak Over Petty, I finally have a nickname.

I flew out to L.A. in 2018 to see my family, but also to catch a show. I told them before I was coming that I was still going to be their roadie, for old time's sake. I might not be able to lift that Marshall stack as easily as I used to, but I was gonna make it happen—no matter what.

The conversation sorta went like this:

Ken: "Hey Meat, Hey Shorty, I'm headed out to L.A. for your Petty show, and I'm gonna be your goddam roadie."

Shorty: "Nice man. That'll help, thanks. Hey Dave, it looks like we got an agent, and a roadie named Bart."

Meat: "Ha, that's great. It'll be good to see you. (Pause) Wait, did Ken just get his nickname?"

Shorty: "You know what, I believe he did."

So, after twenty-five years of helping these bastards out, my grand all-time Rock n Roll nickname is Bart.

And I fucking love it.

I still wish Pincushion Jones would go big, get a song on a movie, and get some airplay or something. If you want to listen to them, call Jess and Dave. I think they still have about a thousand CD's sitting around their garage. I'm sure they'll be more than happy to send you one. Tweet me for the number. Oh, I'm gonna enjoy doing this. This is gonna be fun. Love, Bart.

Chapter 5.2

"Pick Up That Guitar and Play, Just Like Yesterday"

I didn't just work for bands all around L.A. for no money.

I tried starting my own as well, or tried to join others. I really did. I practiced. I took lessons.

I didn't just pick up an electric guitar and learn three chords, like most annoying bands of the '90s (looking at you, 311!). I started with acoustic; I wanted to do it right.

It was a beautiful disaster.

As I mentioned in an earlier chapter, my dad played drums and timpani his whole life, and played them quite well. He played in the official U.S. Army band in England during WWII, and formed a Big Band during the war on his down time. In fact, that band was lucky enough one day to open up for The Glenn Miller Orchestra at the Stage Door Canteen in Piccadilly, London in July 1942. That would be like opening for

Beyoncé today. Those guys were huge. There are some fun, but grainy, videos on You Tube of Glenn's performance that night. I wonder if Dad was there in the audience!

He played in all sorts of clubs in New York and Philadelphia in the '40s, '50s, and '60s. Clubs like the Copacabana and clubs in Harlem. He didn't care; he loved all the music and just wanted to play.

And I wanted to be just like him.

My shot came back in college, when a fraternity brother of mine, who was a great drummer, lost his job, and was about to lose his apartment, so he had to go live in his van to save money—which we conveniently parked on the front lawn of the fraternity house.

Hey, we took care of our own!

But he had a drum set—and a real fine one to boot.

He had a Slingerland Mahogany drum set with two toms, a floor tom, a pair of cymbals, and lots of great Rock n Roll advice!

It was gorgeous. And sounded great. And given his newfound financial predicament, I asked him if I could keep this beautiful set nice and safe for him until he was ready to have it back. He said yes, and I placed it in the only place I could.

Smack in the middle of my college apartment living room, which was about the size of a drum set to begin with.

The look on my roommate's face the day he came home from work was something I'll never forget. But he laughed at me, and was eventually cool with it, so I went off in search of a drum teacher.

I couldn't wait to get started—I was going to rock. I was going to be famous. Girls were going to notice me. Because they always noticed the drummer, right Tommy Lee?

I found a teacher and started lessons—mostly at his house, but with a lot of practice at mine. We started off with basic wrist techniques, a little bit of music theory, a discussion of our favorite drummers (we can debate these in a later chapter—get your lists ready), some early practice techniques like 'paradiddles', and where I wanted this whole music thing to go.

After practicing the basics for a few lessons, we went on to start playing some songs. Very easy drum songs to begin with. "Back in Black," by AC/DC. "Bad Company," by Bad Company. And even "In Bloom," by Nirvana. That one wasn't that easy at first, but it was very repetitive so if I lost my way, I could easily jump right back in a bit later.

We must have played those songs three hundred times each just to get down technique, rhythm, timing, etc.

And I must have played those songs three hundred times at my apartment too. I'm sure there are some people out there still cursing my name. Some people who were trying to study for their chemistry test, get to second base with a member of the opposite sex, or even just trying to sleep.

I can hear them now around their Thanksgiving dinner table: "I used to live in a college apartment where this one asshole played "Back in Black" twelve times a day and man did he suck!"

So, I probably owe them an apology.

But fuck it. I was going to be a rock star drummer.

Rock star drummers don't apologize.

I do hope that every time they hear "Bad Company," they think of me. Well, and the legend that is Paul Rodgers. But, mostly me.

When I finally felt like I could handle this a bit, and gained some musical confidence, a strange thing happened.

Someone wanted me to try out for their band.

Someone I knew was a huge fan of 311 (should have been a red flag right there!) and wanted to try and start a band to see what they could do.

I must have had a frozen-deer-type look on my face because they stopped, looked at me, and asked me again. Then we both laughed.

"Sure, what the fuck, I'll give this a shot," I told him. "I'm not great, but let's have some fun."

We met up at his friend's house a few days later. They played me a song they had written, with a previous drummer, and asked if I could do that.

I sat down, and for the first time ever, I jammed.

They played the song, I tried to remember what I just heard. I riffed a little. I screwed up a lot. We played it again, and a few more times to boot.

This 311-stuff wasn't half bad I thought to myself. This could be a lot of fun—I should totally listen to those guys more often!

But when it was all over, I felt like I was just flat out horrible.

So naturally, I was stunned when the next day they said they wanted me for their band.

"Huh," I asked. "Really?"

"Yeah," my buddy said, "they liked your energy and your willingness to learn and try, so what do you say?"

What a cool fucking thing to say! I was so honored. I still am.

I said no.

I think they got someone else and played locally throughout L.A. for a bit, and then just went their separate ways. Oh, what could have been.

Truthfully, I thought they could do better with someone else. And frankly, I was just a little bit scared—I wasn't ready. I only knew three songs! I wanted more practice and more lessons. I got back to it.

The drum lessons went on for a good five to six months, and then I hit a wall.

It was like I got to level five out of ten on a video game and could never get any further.

My teacher knew I was stuck. We tried more practice, different songs and even song parts—like the opening thirty seconds to "Tom Sawyer" (The song is tough, but that opening is pretty manageable).

We tried using a metronome. I tried learning the "rock shuffle" on drums (think: "I Can't Get Enough of Your Love," by Bad Company, "Rock Forever," by Judas Priest, or even "La Grange" by ZZ Top).

But nothing was working; I couldn't break through the block. I stalled, and still don't know why. It's quite frustrating to me, even twenty-five years later. Was it fear? Was it lack of knowledge or talent? Was I just a total slacker? I really don't have an answer. What do you all think?

Not long after I hit this wall, my fraternity brother got back on his feet, and wanted his lovely drum kit back. And I had to oblige, of course. I drove it back over to him, and my dreams of taking over for Steven Adler at a Guns N Roses show seemingly ended.

But I was not to be deterred.

If I wasn't going to make it as the next Gil Moore or Ginger Baker, then I was going to be the next goddam Jimmy Page.

Bring on the guitar lessons.

I bought my first guitar from a buddy at The Cheesecake Factory. It was an "Imitation Ovation" also known as an Applause. A cheaper-end guitar but it was in good shape, and it looked and sounded pretty good. Plus, he gave me the case, some song books, and an electric tuner as part of the deal. I was so ready.

Thanks to the guys in Pincushion Jones, I got some early free lessons. How to space my fingers across the fret on a C chord, why it's easy to cheat with an A-minor, and how Eddie Van Halen made that cool high-pitched guitar sound at the very opening of "Runnin' With the Devil." Huh, I never knew!

But if I wanted to get some real guitar time, I had to go to the one place in L.A. where the legends were made. Not Guitar Center—although that place was pretty badass. But, being from Santa Monica, you go to McCabe's!

By the time I started taking lessons there, McCabe's was well into its fourth decade of Rock n Roll legend status.

It was started in 1958 by Gerry McCabe—a furniture

designer, who also happened to specialize in acoustic and folk instruments. Soon after, a guy named Bobby Kimmel joined the staff and developed the McCabe's concert series.

Bobby was the first guy to play with a young talent out of Tucson, Arizona named Linda Ronstadt, and was in a ground-breaking band with her called The Stone Poneys. After a while, the record companies just wanted Linda, so she went off to record all the songs we know to this day—which made her a global sensation. Bobby went to work for Jerry and wanted to bring great music to L.A. fans in an intimate setting.

When it comes to concert venues, McCabe's is not very big. I think it holds a hundred fifty to two hundred people—and that's if you're packed in really tightly. There are guitars hanging on every wall imaginable. And in the back, there are practice booths for aspiring Ace Frehley's like me.

If you get a chance, go look at the list of bands that have played McCabe's over the years—REM, Frank Black, Lucinda Williams, Joni Mitchell, and so many more. The list is truly mind-boggling. Whatever your favorite genre of music may be, someone played it at McCabe's.

Also, if you get a chance, go watch that great documentary on Linda Ronstadt called "The Sound of my Voice" on CNN, of all places. It's quite good—the guest stars are fantastic, and the video footage of Linda singing is, well, just sit back and enjoy.

Anyway, I signed up for ten lessons at McCabe's, brought my Applause, and got ready to rock.

Well, not so fast there, buckaroo. First you got to learn how to tune the damn thing. And not with a silly ol' electronic gizmo doodad, but with your very own ears! That took two lessons. Then I had to start with scales. Three more lessons. Then I had to learn to change my strings. One lesson.

Don't get me wrong—any guitar player worth their power chord can tell you that these were all essential skills for a future Eric Clapton, but I wanted to rock, and now—and I was getting a bit impatient.

I begged my teacher to teach me at least one or two rock songs in the first ten lessons. He wanted me to do more scales (he was right!) but eventually gave me some song book material, and I got to learn a few songs.

The first one he pulled out was "Wish You Were Here"—both the strum part and the opening solo acoustic part. The strumming was pretty darn easy. Hey, I was playing guitar, dammit! But that opening solo acoustic part—holy shit. How did David Gilmore do that? Another three lessons were spent practicing just that part.

Looking back, I think my teacher was trying to discourage me from taking the easy road and not learning the instrument the proper way. Once again, he was probably right. He could've started me off on "Smoke on the Water," or some Tom Petty. Something with some simple chord progressions and easy changes during the bridge. But no, he gave me Pink Floyd. Ouch.

He could sense I was struggling, so we did learn a few "easier" songs as well.

"Take it Easy," by The Eagles, "All That I Know," by The Screaming Trees, and even the guitar parts for "Back in Black," but on an acoustic guitar. That just sounded odd to me. So anti-Angus. But okay, I'll try anything.

I had one lesson left of my pre-paid package.

Was it going to be "Photograph," by Def Leppard, or some cool Roy Orbison track, or maybe even some fucking Metallica!

Nope, we didn't even take the guitar out of the case. We just talked.

We talked theory, and bands, and the history of guitar, and what he liked, and what I liked. I honestly think he was stoned that day. We just chatted, like two old friends who used to work on a Def Leppard road crew thirty years ago, comparing our favorites and talking about life.

I never took another lesson again. I was frustrated, and wanted to move on to something else. Job. School. Dating. Anything else. That was it.

It's funny, these days, if you pull up next to me at a light or step onto the treadmill next to mine, I'm usually playing some monster drum solo on my steering wheel or contorting my fingers in the air to a kick ass Iron Maiden guitar solo, as if I know what the fuck I'm actually doing. I don't—but I don't care.

The music is in there somewhere, and that's my way of getting it out. Don't think I'm a poser or someone trying to look cooler than he is—I'm not. Just throw up some metal horns, or these days, take a video of me for Tik Tok, and just rock on by.

B-sides

A few other quick notes about trying anything I could to get involved with music.

- A buddy of mine from the A&M days was on the road crew for the Def Leppard "In the Round In Your Face" tour of 1998 to support the *Hysteria* album. Damn, that was a fun tour. He invited me backstage after their concert at the L.A. Forum that year. We chatted, caught up, had a few drinks. Gene Simmons was three feet from me! But anyway, then he asked me if I wanted to join the crew! Holy fucking shit! They were my favorite band! But, for some reason, I said, 'give me a day' and he said, 'cool, if you decide to do it, meet us in Phoenix tomorrow, we'll add you to the roster, and put you to work. Get ready for Rock n Roll, baby.' I got home, told some friends, and thought about it. And then said no. I was halfway through my MBA program and didn't want to pause and start over. I've had a decent career because of that MBA so I can't complain, but, like the earlier job offer in the A&M studio booth, I always wondered 'what could have been.'

- I worked for one summer at GNP Crescendo Records on the Sunset Strip. This time, for actual money! But it was only a summer gig. Crescendo started in the '50s as a jazz label, but when I worked there, it was famous for its really weird sci-fi stuff. In fact, their biggest claim to fame was obtaining the rights to release the soundtracks for all the *Star Trek* movies. They had booths at all the Trekkie conventions, and these fans really bought the music! "Dude, you got the soundtrack to Star Trek 4, that's so much better than Star Trek 3." They were a small office, and the money wasn't great, so there wasn't a lot of opportunity for moving up, but I'm grateful for the experience of working in the record business—even for a short time.

- It was around this time in my life that my mom got remarried too, to a cool L.A. guy named Jack. Goofy, fun, smart, and really into music, Jack was just wild to be around. I'll admit it took me a while to warm up to him, but I've seen how happy he makes my mom and that's all I could ever hope for. Well, Jack had two stepsons, Carlos and Celso, who were in a cool band that I'd already heard about, called Possum Dixon. They had one decent hit on the alternative radio stations of the world, like KROQ in L.A., called "Watch That Girl Destroy Me." Those guys were a lot of fun and really good live musicians. I think one of their albums was produced by Ric Ocasek of The Cars fame. So, they had some legitimate talent in their corner. Anyway, they toured all over and I was really hoping to do something with them in another attempt to work with or for a band coming out of L.A.. Unfortunately, Celso ended up with a bad bout of pneumonia, which ended up taking his life. I only got to hang with him a little bit and I wish it could have been more. He was super-talented and will be missed.

- Not a job story, but during the year I was taking drum lessons, I did find myself at a party one day at the house of GNR drummer, Steven Adler. His brother was a buddy of mine for a short time. He knew I played drums and loved the band, so he invited me over. I got to meet Steven briefly–very cool dude–and I asked him If I could go downstairs to his studio and sit on this drum set for a bit. "Yeah man, enjoy" are the three words he said that I'll never forget. I went down there, passed a few people who were just staring at the set, and sat down. The room looked at me like I was fucking insane. His brother laughed and said 'don't worry, my brother said he could" so I got out some sticks and played for about a minute. On Steven Adler's drum set. The one he used to make *Appetite for Destruction*. Pinch me. Still gives me goosebumps.

McCABE'S
GUITAR
SHOP

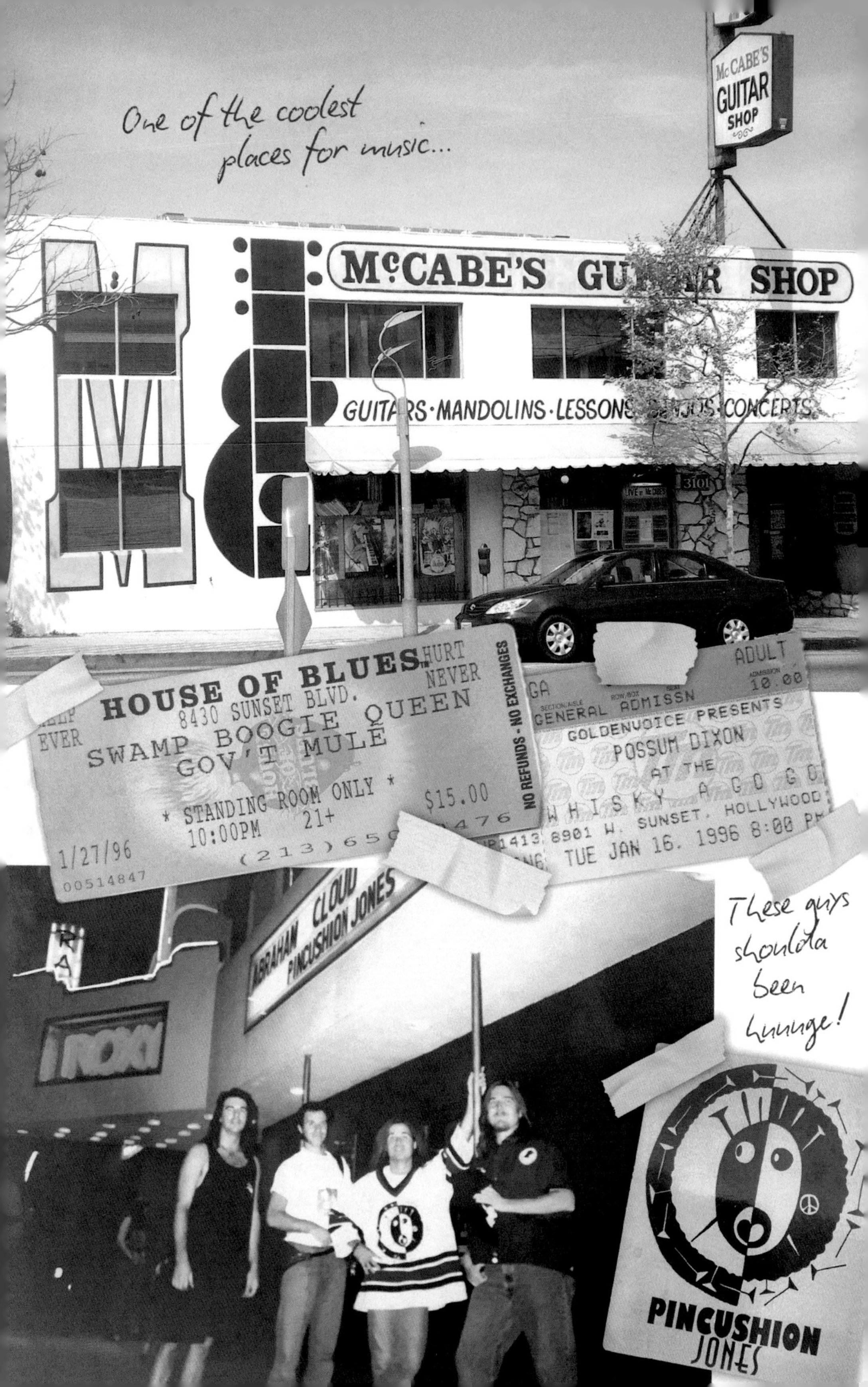
One of the coolest places for music...
McCABE'S GUITAR SHOP
McCABE'S GUITAR SHOP
GUITARS · MANDOLINS · LESSONS · CONCERTS
3101
HOUSE OF BLUES
HURT NEVER
8430 SUNSET BLVD.
SWAMP BOOGIE QUEEN
GOV'T MULE
* STANDING ROOM ONLY *
$15.00
10:00PM 21+
1/27/96
00514847
NO REFUNDS - NO EXCHANGES
ADULT
10.00
GENERAL ADMISSN
GOLDENVOICE PRESENTS
POSSUM DIXON
AT THE
WHISKY A GO GO
8901 W. SUNSET, HOLLYWOOD
TUE JAN 16, 1996 8:00 PM
ABRAHAM CLOUD
PINCUSHION JONES
ROXY
These guys shoulda been huuuge!
PINCUSHION JONES

I annoyed the hell
out of my neighbors
with this set

PolyGram

Pink Elephant
Bong Load!
Oh, I
mean Munkafust

MUNKAFUST

Ch

RISE UP, GATHER ROUND, ROCK THIS PLACE TO THE GROUND

apter 6

"Rise Up, Gather Round, Rock This Place, To the Ground"

Why You Should Go to as Many Shows as Possible and Why You Should Never, Ever Grab the Stump

I worked in the business and worked for bands. I took some lessons, but it didn't work. Or I wasn't good enough. Or both. And that's okay–it was time to move on. But one thing I never stopped being, was a fan. Let's get back to the music, shall we? That's what this whole book is about.

Growing up in L.A. was a lot of fun. Every band played there, and a lot of them lived there. Just about every wannabe band tried to make it there. It made for some excellent Rock n Roll moments throughout my life.

Like walking down Melrose Ave and seeing Perry Ferrell from Jane's Addiction come out of a thrift store. So that's where he got all his stage clothes! Going to Dinah's Family Restaurant on the corner of Sepulveda and Centinela and seeing Scott Ian from Anthrax eating his pancakes like everyone else in this famous West L.A. Diner.

Or perhaps having too many shots of something one night–hint: it rhymes with "Kläger Neister"–and convincing a friend to drive us all around the Hollywood Hills in search of the house of Axl Rose. She was in love with Axl, so it wasn't hard to convince her. And let's be honest—I love him as a Rock n Roll front man, but we were going to find his house, knock on his door, and invite ourselves in. I mean, I played on Steven Adler's drum set for fifty-seven seconds, how could Axl not pour us a drink?

We never found his house. Remember, there was no Internet then, and my *Thomas Guide* didn't exactly point out the homes of famous rock stars. So, we ended up at a taco truck outside some club at three in the morning, and rocked to *Use Your Illusion* the entire time. Both I and II, thank you very much!

But these were the kinds of silly opportunities you just don't have in most major American cities. And this nexus of Rock n Roll is what brought all the good concerts to Los Angeles. Many of which, I hope to describe here.

Chapter 6.1

"Too Much Magic Bus"

The '90s and '00s were a blur of concerts for me. I wanted to go to every concert I could afford and see every type or style of band that was coming through town. Try new things, and take recommendations from friends.

You heard that the band playing at Dragonfly on a Tuesday night was good? I'm so there.

And because it was always a dream to find 'the next big thing', I went to every club show I could find in the hopes of seeing the modern-day equivalent of "The Doors" before they left the Whiskey a-Go-Go and became international superstars.

When those shows came to town, my friends and I were always willing to go that extra mile to make this happen.

The Glen Helen Blockbuster Pavilion (which later became the San Manuel Amphitheater after Blockbuster went belly-up, and then became the Glen Helen Amphitheater) is located, oddly enough, in the Glen Helen Regional Park in San Bernardino,

California (roughly seventy-plus miles east of where I grew up). Which, if you know anything about L.A., could take anywhere from one to thirty-seven hours to get to.

But Glen Helen lists itself as the largest outdoor music venue in the United States, and can seat roughly sixty-five thousand music fans in chairs and up through the hill sides of the park. As a comparison, the world-famous Red Rocks Park and Amphitheater, in Morrison, CO—the one in U2's famous Sunday Bloody Sunday video, and a place I'm dying to see a show—can only hold nine-thousand five-hundred.

So, needless to say, not only was this place massive, but also in the fucking boonies for West L.A. scum such as myself.

There was no way me, or any of my friends, would be able to drive there, drink, rock out, and then drive back, without some help—or a serious traffic-related aneurysm. But we had a plan.

In early 1996, L.A. Rock n Roll radio station KLOS announced a free show, coming on July 6th, called "Independence Daze" (get it?). This show would have The Black Crowes, supported by Son Volt, Seven Mary Three, and 3 Lb. Thrill. That's a strong line up for any mid-'90s rock fan.

You could call in and win tickets, write in and ask for some, or stop by the station. Again, remember, nothing to click—since Al Gore had yet to grace us with his greatest invention: the Internet.

I sent away for tickets the first moment I could.

My buddy Jess from Pincushion Jones did too.

Well, turns out that ten more of our friends did this as well.

All of a sudden, we had about thirty tickets to see this show. This was going to rock.

But back to the problem of transportation: We couldn't get all thirty of us there safely.

What to do?

We rented a bus.

I know this isn't a revelation for most serious concert-goers; I know we weren't the first to do it. And I'm sure many of you have much more sordid tales to tell about your bus concert experience (and I want to read them all!).

But for us, this was new. And it was fun.

So we all got together, and set about the task of coming up with the bus rules.

We weren't going to just get on the bus, ride to the concert, rock out, and come back, were we? Uh, hell no.

Now, I probably don't remember all the rules. And anybody that was on this bus with me can correct me—it's totally fine. I had a lot of drinks that day. Obviously, I was never great at following rules. But here's what I remember:

1. To get on the bus, you must do one jello shot (ah, the '90s!)
2. If you get off the bus before it moves, you must do one jello shot getting off the bus, and then see Rule #1.
3. If you complained about the music, or the volume, you do another jello shot.
4. At any point of the trip, to use the restroom in the back of the bus, you must do one shot of Jack Daniels or Southern Comfort on your way in, and one shot of the other on the way out.
5. If you threw up, you must do two shots of each.
6. If you fell asleep or passed out on the way to the show, you would be written on in sharpie by everyone else on the bus and paraded through the concert venue parade style to show off your new 'tattoos'.
7. For ladies, if you flashed anyone on the freeway on the way to the show, you would receive extra beer at the venue.
8. For men, if you did that, beer would be taken away.
9. No "Mooning" allowed at any point—no one wants to see that, like, ever.
10. If you fell asleep on the way home, no penalties would apply, but if you didn't—please shut the fuck up so the rest of us could chill.

As I said, I'm sure there were more, and I'm sure we invented some stupid ones on the spot. "Oh, you said the word 'Music,' here do a shot" or something ridiculous like that. But those were the basic ground rules—or, the ones I can recall.

Oh yeah, the show. Wow, what a great concert. I love the Black Crowes—always have. I know it's an acquired taste for some people, and that's fine. They rocked it that night and left all sixty-five thousand free ticket holding concert-goers very satisfied, from what I could tell.

And the opening bands were solid too. 3 Lb. Thrill was good, although I think they only had one minor hit and sort of disappeared, I'm not quite sure. Seven Mary Three's first album was always enjoyable, and "Cumbersome" is still a fun hit to bang your head to on the '90s Channel on Sirius XM. And Son Volt was just excellent.

Formed after the breakup of Uncle Tupelo—a band that got a lot of critical attention—Son Volt had a great hit with "Drown" and even more critical acclaim on their future albums. Looking back, they were easily the most talented guys on stage that night, and no doubt the best songwriters—so seeing them for free was a total treat.

And for those of you curious about the ride home, no one made a goddamn sound.

Another great concert adventure happened the previous summer. Pearl Jam and Bad Religion were playing a concert at Golden Gate Park, the Polo Fields, which could hold roughly fifty-five thousand people. This would be my first time seeing Pearl Jam, and there was no way I would miss that.

So, in late June of 1995, my buddy Michelle and I piled in her car and headed north, up the awful 5 Freeway to get to the Bay Area. Los Angeles and San Francisco are wonderful cities and California is my home state, but the drive between those two cities on the 5 is nothing but truck stops and brown hills, and you just can't get to your destination fast enough.

We stayed at her friend's house and woke up early to get to the Polo Fields so we could get a good spot for Pearl Jam.

Fifty thousand other fans had the same idea.

At last, we plopped our blanket down about a hundred feet away from the second set of video screens, and set about to enjoy the show. The stage was so far away, it looked like one of those red hotels you can purchase in Monopoly.

But the vibe was cool, and the weather was perfect. The fans were all happy–dancing, drinking, smoking, and just having a good time.

Bad Religion–one of the coolest, and smartest, punk bands of all time–put on a great opening act. Recipe for Hate came out in 1993, which got them some radio play for their great song, "It Struck a Nerve," and Stranger Than Fiction came out in 1994, which got them massive radio play for "Infected," and "21st Century Digital Boy."

"There's an infant clinging
To his overweight mother in the cold
As they go to shop for cigarettes
And she spends her last dollar
On a bottle of vodka for tonight
And I guess it struck a nerve"

Holy shit. Who writes stuff like this? Bad Religion, that's who! Monster song. Gut punch of a message, and a totally kick-ass pair of albums to boot.

Then the crowd got revved up for Eddie and the boys. They came on stage and crushed it.

Last Exit, Spin the Black Circle, Go, Animal, Tremor Christ, Corduroy, Not For You.

What a way to start a fucking rock show!

Many people up front rushed the stage. The people near us in the back put down their funny-smelling cigarettes and started dancing, singing–and okay–smoking too. Let's be honest here–it was a perfect way to spend the weekend, and the perfect way to rock.

Until Eddie left.

Apparently, Mr. Vedder had a bad case of the flu—or stomach flu, or what it was I'm still not really quite sure. But he went off stage and got sick. Horribly 'I can't move' type of sick. Poor dude.

There is no hatred in this statement. The man was sick and still came out and did a rocking show, for seven songs, and I will forever love him for that.

But, like many of my compatriots in the field that day, I drove seven hours to see a show and seven songs just wasn't going to cut it. And they knew that. So, they had a backup plan.

Neil Young was backstage and was planning to come out and do some songs with them later in the set. Neil and Pearl Jam played together a lot in those days. I think Pearl Jam considered Neil "the godfather of grunge" or something, which makes sense, I suppose. But regardless, they enjoyed each other's musical company, played on each other's albums, showed up at various charities together, and otherwise just had a damn good time rocking out.

Stone or Jeff from Pearl Jam broke the bad news to the crowd.

"Eddie is really sick and just not able to perform anymore for you today, we're so sorry, we love you, and we still want to play for you, so thank you for your understanding" or something similar to that. It was a very apologetic message. Sick happens. It wasn't Eddie's fault—we all came to enjoy ourselves, so let's move on.

Not everyone saw it that way.

A lot of the crowd started booing. Some started throwing food and beer cups and other trash.

Others headed for the door.

At some point, Stone got on the mic and rebuked the crowd a bit for their attitude and for what they were seeing, which prompted cheers from those of us who planned to stay. And we're so glad we did.

Neil was just about to release his 21st studio album, *Mirrorball*, which is simply phenomenal. He came out on stage and, with Pearl Jam as his backing band, played some songs from his new album. I want to pause and repeat that—he had Pearl Jam, one of the hottest bands on the planet at the time, as his backup band. That's fucking cool!

He also did a bunch of his classic hits as well, including "The Needle and the Damage Done," "Down by the River," and of course, "Keep on Rockin' in the Free World."

It was not a bad way to play songs of your new album for the first time. The crowd that stayed was very appreciative they did that. They didn't have to; they could've dialed it in and went home, using Eddie's flu as an excuse. But they knew what we were there to see, and if they couldn't give us the set they wanted, they gave us the set we got.

And, if I'm being honest, thanks to half the crowd that left early, getting out of the city and heading home wasn't that bad either!

Chapter 6.2

"It's Time To Fly the Finger"

Somewhere in the middle of all these epic adventures, I found, and fell in love with, one band more than any other.

Yes, I will forever love Led Zeppelin, and Guns N' Roses, and Pearl Jam, and my first love—Def Leppard. But this was different. This was a band I 'discovered' with my friends. This was the band that was going to rise from the depths of the L.A. club scene, take over the world, and allow me to say to everyone I ever met, 'yeah, whatever, I used to see those guys in small L.A. clubs, I'm so cool.' And have everyone think I was this Rock n Roll savant. Or a complete asshole. Either way. But these guys were the ones.

I've come a long way with my cockiness, haven't I?

They billed themselves as "The World's Greatest Rock n Roll Band (just ask them)" and I just thought that was the coolest marketing campaign ever. But the music was even better.

The Supersuckers started in Tucson, Arizona and then made their way to Seattle in the late '80s or early '90s. Not so much—according to their old website—to be a part of the famous "Seattle Scene", but rather to just get the fuck out of Tucson!

My best friend Erik still lives in Tucson. He couldn't agree with the Supersuckers anymore if he tried!

These guys have all the swagger of bonafide rock stars. The Stones. UFO. Motorhead. Nashville Pussy. These guys are in that group. The rock they put right in your face is a night well spent.

They have two-three minutes songs. Short, sharp hooks. Monster guitar solos, usually on a Les Paul Gold Top guitar, quite possibly the best guitar ever invented, and they have a bass player, Mr. Eddie Spaghetti, with a great voice, awesome lyrics, and a "I really don't give a fuck what you think, son" kind of attitude.

If you can't rock out to a guy called Eddie Spaghetti, then you can't rock out at all.

Since I can't really relay them to you properly in a book, I implore you to go put on songs like "Doublewide" or "She's My Bitch," "Creepy Jackelope Eye," "Hell City, Hell," my personal favorite, "Marie," or everybody's favorite, "Born With A Tail."

It's time to fly that finger
Yeah, that middle digit brings its point
And drives it home

Great shit.

I hope the e-book version of this story has links right to these videos. And I hope that one night, you're laying in bed, and you click on that link, and this roaring music comes out of your device, and your wife wakes up and punches you in the face and yells 'go the fuck to sleep!' That sums up the power of the Rock n Roll that you get with The Supersuckers.

But The Supersuckers have a couple other sides to them as well.

First, is their alt-country style of music. They truly appreciate country music and try and recreate some great songs while creating some of their own, using their own personal brand of swagger in every note. They've played with great old and current country talent, and have put out numerous albums with just alt-country hits.

If you get a second, put on "Road Worn and Weary," which, in my opinion, needs to be on every country radio station in the U.S., and in cool road-themed movies to boot. I can totally see Thelma & Louise driving down the road and shooting up gas stations with this song playing in the background. Maybe they'll use it on *Thelma & Louise 2*, since you know Hollywood, long bereft of unique ideas, is going to find a way to make a sequel.

They also did an incredibly kick-ass cover of "Bloody Mary Morning" by Willie Nelson, with Willie singing and playing guitar on the song! The guitar solo in that song is totally worth your time. The Supersuckers are in the background grinding at a hundred miles per hour while Willie is gently picking away at his six-string the way he likes to do it, totally showing the boys how it's done. I would've given a lot of money to be in the studio that day, just to hear the words of wisdom handed down from one generation of legends to another. Love ya Willie—don't ever change.

You've got the rock. You've got the country. Then there is the fun side of the Supersuckers.

First, they don't take themselves too seriously, and have written some pretty non-PC funny-ass songs like "How To Maximize Your Kill Count" and "The Supersucker Drive-by

Blues," the latter of which is an ode to Van Halen's "Ice Cream Man." Ode? It's a genuine rip-off, but like the Van Halen classic, it's fun as hell to listen to.

Yes, readers, I realize that some of these song titles, and song lyrics are not very politically correct. They aren't 'woke'—whatever the fuck that means—and they sure as hell aren't very #MeToo, but for fuck's sake, it's Rock n Roll, people. If you want 'woke,' go listen to another channel.

Second, during their song "Born With a Tail," which is usually their encore, and has that great set of song lyrics which I wrote above, they actively encourage the entire audience to flip them off. I can't recall ever seeing hundreds of people flipping off a band and them being super excited about it. But something about doing that just feels so right at a Supersuckers concert.

By the way, how do you flip people off? Do you use the whole finger, or do you bend your first and ring finger to form a set of 'mountains' around your middle finger? I hate the mountain way. If I'm gonna flip someone off, they're gonna get every glorious inch of my middle digit. If I'm ever lucky enough to do a book signing for this book, or some other public appearance, please come see me and tell me how you do it, and why. Or better yet, just show me. The bookstore manager will freak out!

Finally, the Supersuckers created, what I consider to be, one of the greatest live moments in Rock n Roll—the fake encore.

We've all gone to shows. The band finishes up their set but they haven't quite played "Pour Some Sugar on Me," or "Back in Black," or "Even Flow" just yet. You know it's coming. They know it's coming. And thanks to apps like SetList.fm, everybody in the building knows it's coming.

But the band says thank you to the crowd. You were so lovely this evening. We'll be back next year. Blah Blah Blah. They walk off the stage, but curiously, the lights in the arena stay dark. No one leaves for the exits (except those people who want to beat traffic and guess which finger I have for those people—see above for every glorious inch of my middle digit). Then three minutes later, the band miraculously returns, as if pulled back on stage by the cheers and applause and sheer charm of the audience before them. "We were gonna leave, Kansas City, but you lovely fans brought us back on stage!"

Yeah, okay.

Instead of doing all that shit, The Supersuckers created the "fake encore, patent pending," as Eddie likes to say.

"We'll pretend to walk off the stage, you pretend to cheer us back on, we'll pretend we did it just for you, and then we'll just keep on playing."

Perfect.

So, most every Supersuckers show ends this way, and instead of wasting three minutes, they have time for one or two more songs. And more time for everyone to stick their middle finger in the air and show the boys just how they really feel.

It's been twenty-five years since I saw them for the first time at The Viper Room, on Sunset—a great club, unfortunately made famous by the death of River Phoenix. But, by now, I've seen The Supersuckers twenty six or more times—on both coasts. And they still just bring it hard every night.

As I mentioned, I've seen lots of bands in small clubs over the years—I know you have too. But I wanted to highlight The Supersuckers in particular to describe the raw power of lesser-known bands who are trying really hard. They're out there, every night, working their ass off to entertain you, to play great music, and okay—to get famous and tour the world, meet chicks, drink free beer, and open for Van Halen. And you know what—there is nothing wrong with that.

Go out and see one this weekend. Enjoy it—you deserve it. And if The Supersuckers are coming through your town, you better go see them too.

Even Lemmy, from Motorhead, once said: "If you don't like

The Supersuckers, you don't like Rock n Roll." And are you gonna ignore Lemmy? Yeah, I thought not.

Chapter 6.3

"Let it Rock, Let it Roll, Let it Go"

I've documented often in this book how Def Leppard is 'my' band. The one that will always be #1 in my heart. The one that got me into Rock n Roll and heavy metal. And the one I will probably always pay to see even if they tour with curious non-'80s metal acts like Journey or Bryan Adams or Cheap Trick (all great shows by the way).

Def Leppard has provided so many great music moments in life. Not just seeing them live in concert—which I've done sixteen times—at the writing of this book, with tickets for the Def Leppard-Motley Crüe-Poison-Joan Jett concert sitting right next to me as I type!

But also, for all the things I've done while *listening* to Def Leppard. All the rooms I've painted. All the road trips I've taken. All the books I've read. All the tests I've studied for. All the ladies I... wished...I dated. They've been there for all of it.

So, it should come as no surprise that Def Leppard is the source of one of my greatest musical moments of all time—and the source of my greatest embarrassment.

Wait, you thought that time talking baseball with Whitney Houston was bad? Oh, silly readers, sit back and enjoy.

On May 9th, 1996, Def Leppard was going to do a live worldwide album release party for their new CD, Slang. Los Angeles radio station KLOS was going to broadcast it and, I found out later, simulcast it on over 144 radio stations around the world.

They were going to perform songs from the new album, take questions from the KLOS DJ, "Uncle" Joe Benson, take questions from the audience, and just generally have a damn good time playing Rock n Roll.

And they were doing this live in the backyard of the Zeta Beta Tau (ZBT) Fraternity at UCLA.

Huh?

Yup.

Was their manager a ZBT from back in the day? Was there a connection to the radio station? Did ZBT brothers send in enough box tops to win this amazing opportunity, and a free oven mitt from Pillsbury? To this day, I'm still not sure of how that came about. But it was happening.

No tickets were issued for the event. Just industry insiders, and drunk UCLA fraternity boys, allowed. What could go wrong?

I called every contact I had in the record world. All my friends at A&M, who had contacts at Polygram, who knew people at Q Prime—the agency of Peter Mensch and Cliff Burnstein, who helped manage Def Leppard. I believe that is how I got my name on the list to get in.

I was so fucking stoked.

I was going to see my Rock n Roll heroes. And they were going to be right there. Right there in front of me. Five feet maybe? Ten? Didn't matter. Whatever it was, it was significantly better than being twelve rows from the back at the L.A. Forum, or too far away to mention on the lawn at Jiffy Lube Live in Bristow, Virginia. When they sang "Photograph," they were gonna hear me singing right along with them. This was gonna be legendary.

The day comes and we all head to Westwood to see the show. The ZBT's had a nice house. Nothing spectacular, but it was cool. And they had a nice backyard. Again, nothing you'd see on HGTV, but still cool nonetheless. Except today it was packed with about five hundred people.

I was a frat boy; I knew how it worked. But I had never been to a ZBT house in my life to that point, so I'm sure they had parties there all the time and the backyard was similarly packed. But this was just nuts. No one could move. Had to go the bathroom? Good luck, pal. And there was barely enough room to lift my beer to my mouth, but, gosh darnit—I was gonna try.

The band came out, along with Uncle Joe, some sound guys, some video guys, and a few other assorted people.

Uncle Joe did his thing and introduced the band, talked about the new album, the recording process, the songs, and covered a little bit of Def Leppard history—including how Rick Allen was playing acoustic drums again, and how newer member Vivian Campbell contributed to the song writing process.

We were warned to be polite, not swear, cheer loudly when appropriate, and just generally have a good time. If we didn't do any of those things, we would be invited to leave, and quickly, by the large beefy security men KLOS had brought along with them.

During the interviews, the boys played one cut off their new album, "Work It Out," a damn fine song. Some additional non-live album cuts from Slang were played on air as well, including "All I Want is Everything," "Turn to Dust," and "Gift of Flesh," among others.

The interview ended and the show ended. And the KLOS team stopped recording.

But Def Leppard wanted to show their appreciation, so they decided to rock out a little more, just for the folks who happened to be there. The place exploded (we weren't live on air anymore, so who cared, right?). Then they played "Rocket," "Armageddon It," and "Pour Some Sugar on Me," off *Hysteria*, all of which made the crowd go wild.

Thank you, boys, that was great, time to go home and chill, right?

Nope.

They stuck around and wanted to hang with the people. They grabbed a beer, walked into the crowd, shook hands, and chatted us up. "Oh, you saw us in 1983, that's cool." They treated us like normal humans; they just didn't want to go.

There were a few radio VIPs, some record company and management personnel, and even some other rock stars in the crowd–like Bruce Kulick from KISS, and Hugh McDonald from Bon Jovi. Joe, Rick, Phil, Viv, and Sav did hang out and chat with these folks a little more than the rest of us, but nobody cared. I was standing eighteen inches away from Joe and Bruce when they hugged it out and started chatting about what a great show that was. I was part of that conversation!

"Hey Ken, what do you think about KISS' latest direction?"

"Well, Bruce, buddy, let me tell you..."

Okay that only happened in my head, but you know what I mean.

While mingling with the crowd, the guys were also very generous when it came to taking photos with their fans, many of which I have included in this chapter. I even gave my camera to Joe while he was on stage on a break and he took a great crowd shot, with yours truly, which I made the cover of this whole book! All credit to Joe Elliot for his amazing photography skills.

Back then, I had one of those little Kodak disposable cameras that were all the rage.

I know these things weren't environmentally friendly, but they were cheap and easy and took pretty decent pictures for a backyard Rock n Roll concert with your heroes.

This was the camera I handed to Joe when I asked him to take that photo. And this was the camera I used to take all the shots you see here today.

But back in 1996, you didn't get to see them right away. You had no idea if they would turn out. Or if someone's eyes were closed. If someone had crossed your path right as you clicked open the shutter.

You had to take these cameras to a developer–some store that specialized in photos, or sold camera equipment, or one of those little booths in the corner of a parking lot, or even a

Rite-Aid—and pay them to get your photos—which you would receive, usually three-four days later.

For those three-four days, I probably annoyed the ever-loving shit out of everyone I knew. All my co-workers at MGM, and all my friends from the Cheesecake Factory were regaled with the encounter. I think I even called my grandmother in Olympia, WA to tell her about it, and her first response was "deaf who?"

I didn't care. That was one of the best nights of my life, and everyone was going to hear about it.

And I was going to do it all over again too, when I got those photos.

I drove back to Rite-Aid to pick up my shots, paid for them, and ran out the store to my car, like some kid who just got the one baseball card he needed to complete his set.

I enjoyed every moment of those photos.

"Look, there's Joe on stage. He was singing "Work It Out". That's the chorus. Phil is playing a C chord in the background."

"Oh wow, there's Viv and Phil doing their 'dual guitar' thing—damn those guys are so cool."

"Is that Uncle Joe talking to Sav—those two guys are totally badass."

"Oh, look here's me and my metal drummer hero, Rick Allen…"

Oh shit.

Let me back up a second.

Everyone reading this should know the story of Rick Allen—how he started with Def Leppard when he was sixteen and got into a horrible car accident on New Year's Eve 1984 near Sheffield, England. How he lost his left arm in the accident but Def Leppard refused to kick him out of the band, instead waiting years while he re-learned the drums with an electronic—and now acoustic—drum kit. The courage and conviction of all parties to let that happen was incredible. And he's still known as the Thunder God.

It's one of the best stories in Rock n Roll history. It's part of the lore of Def Leppard. And it's a huge reason they are my favorites of all time. They never gave up on him, and he never gave up on them. And they've created some of the best songs in the history of music from that moment forward.

Hysteria alone had seven hit singles!

I was so giddy to meet him. I couldn't believe he was talking to me. I couldn't believe even more that he was cool taking a picture with me.

So, I handed off the camera to whomever was standing next to me, and asked them to take a shot of me and my hero. The drummer—and person—I wanted to be.

We got next to each other and took the shot. I shook his hand, thanked him for everything he did, and we both went about our day.

Fast forward to the Rite Aid parking lot.

I'm standing there looking at that photo.

With my arm around Rick.

And my hand grabbing his stump.

Fuck me.

I think I scared some people in the parking lot that day. I'm sure I cursed loudly. I'm sure I snorted with laughter. I'm sure I was as red as a tomato. That happens when I get embarrassed, which of course—makes me even more embarrassed.

But regardless, I was so mad at myself. So bummed that I turned that epic moment into one of shame. I'm an idiot, I'm sorry, and I felt like a really bad person. I felt wrong.

I hope you can understand this—you just don't do this to a person. Someone who lost a part of themselves like that—and someone you admire so much.

Friends told me I was making too big of a deal about this. And they may be right—you might agree with them, and that's okay. But I felt awful.

I buried that photo for quite a few years. I showed all the photos, except that one, to everyone that would stop and listen. I talked about everything that happened that day, except that moment.

For a long time, that moment didn't exist.

As a fan of the band, I kept up with their music as well as their side projects and charities. And I would read and watch just about any interview on the guys I could find.

Years later, one quote from Rick, when asked about the accident, caught my attention.

"Before my accident I was a little too... selfish and self-absorbed and for me, to now be at the place where I can kinda give back and inspire people. I'm blessed. I'm really blessed."

Damn.

He turned his whole worldview around. His accident wasn't a curse; it was a blessing. A blessing to him, and his friends and family. And of course—a blessing to his fans.

I have absolutely no right to compare myself to a man like this, but I did think, in that moment, that if he saw himself that way, then I could be okay with grabbing the man's stump!

Years later I found that photo again. And couldn't stop laughing. Not at what I did, but at myself. How badly I took it all. How big a deal I thought it was, and how silly I was being.

I thought of his quote and his attitude and changed my whole view as well.

I showed off that photo to a few close friends.

They thought I was an idiot—and hey still do. But that's okay.

Now it's part of my Rock n Roll history too. Now I just talk about the show, being five feet from my metal heroes, and hanging with Rick—for a little while, at least.

And hey, it was a really cool show.

At this point, I'm going to take a page here and give Rick a little shout-out for some of his non-Def Leppard endeavors. It's the least I can do, right?

I'm sure he does a lot more, but since I follow everything Def Leppard, these are the two things I wanted to highlight.

First, is Rick's involvement with The Raven Drum Foundation and The Project Resiliency. The Project Resiliency website lists its mission "to serve, educate and empower veterans and people in crisis. To support, promote, and contribute to global healing, multicultural unification, and community leadership."

So badass. How can you oppose any of that!

Rick and his wife founded the organization in 2001 as a way to help people heal. Drum circles. Interventions. Discussions. Whatever it takes. Rick uses his traumatic event, and his worldwide fame, to help others—and he doesn't ask for anything in return.

Mind. Body. Drum.

An incredibly worthy cause, if you have a need to support one.

The second is Rick Allen's art.

To be honest, this one kind of pisses me off. He's such a talented drummer—true rockstar, as well as a true humanist. And he can do art like this with one arm? Screw you, Rick!

Just kidding.

Rick has hooked up with The Wentworth Gallery to create some amazing artwork. He has toured the world showing it off, selling some pieces, and raising more money for his charities. Some are Rock n Roll inspired. Some are inspired by life. But they are all just wonderful, and I wanted to give him a little shout-out here since it's my book and I can do whatever the fuck I want.

Love ya, Rick. You're a true inspiration.

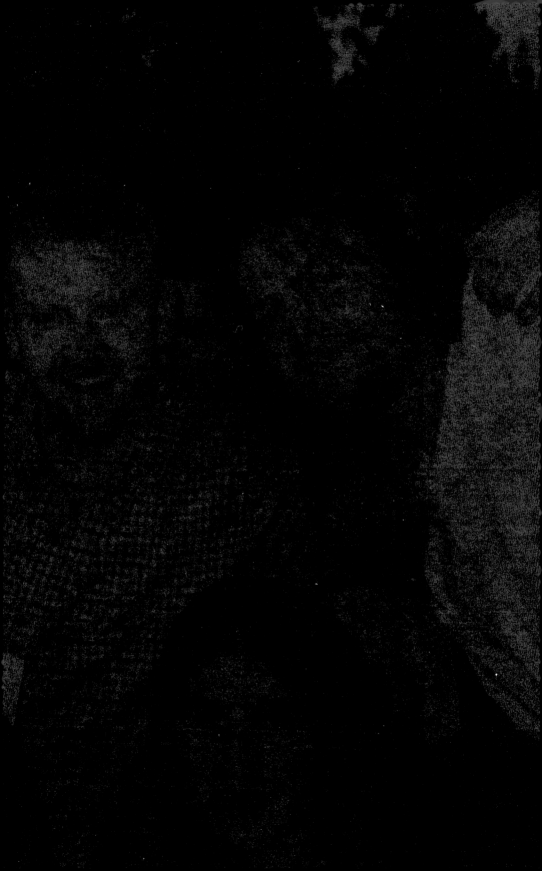

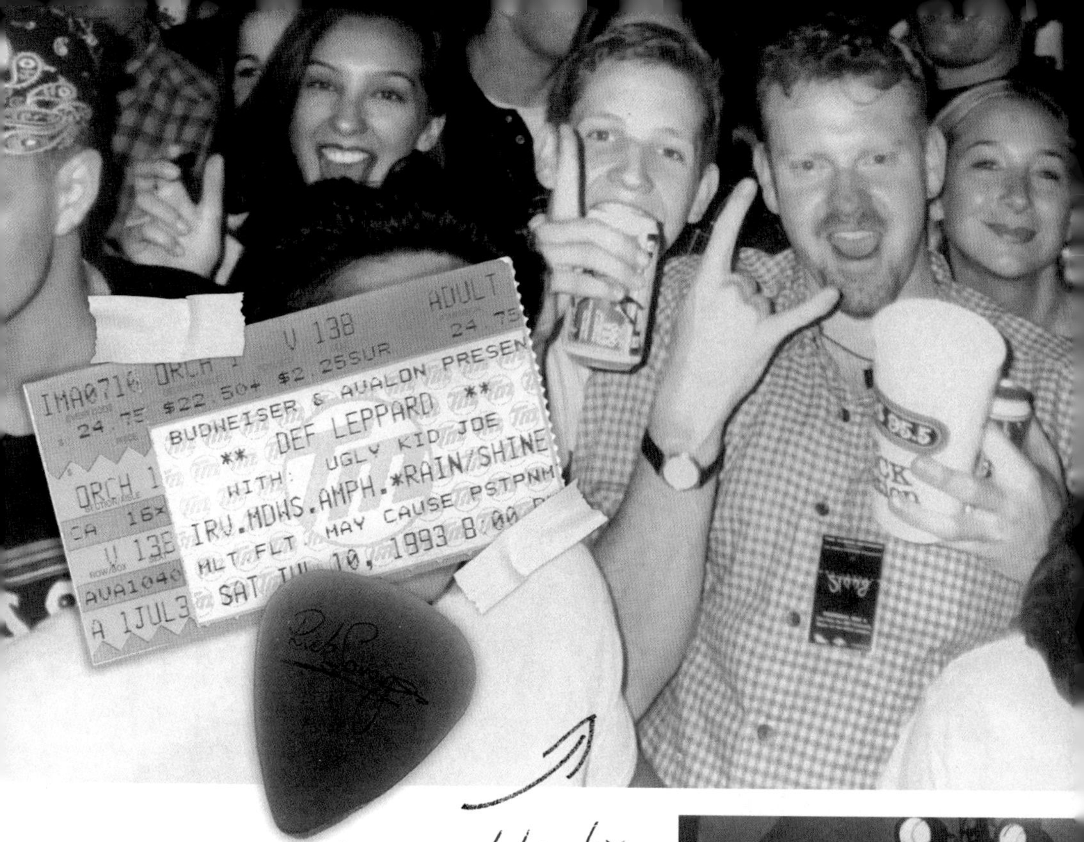

This awesome picture was taken by THE Joe Elliot himslelf! (so it had to be on the cover!)

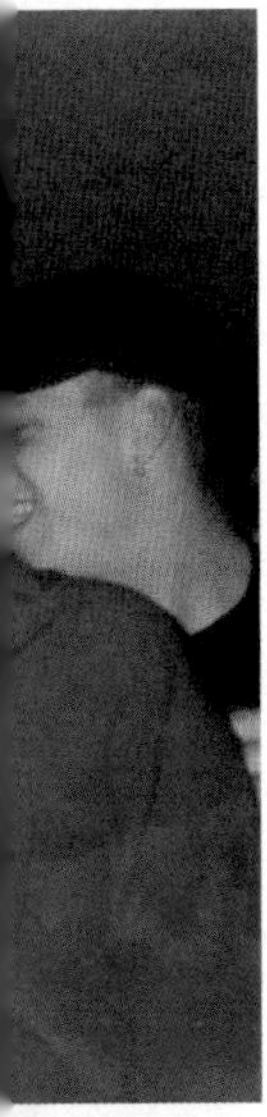

I was born with a tail...

GA0 4 ADULT
WY1030 GA SECTION/AISLE ROW/BOX SEAT ADMISSION 15.00
EVENT CODE GENERAL ADMISSN
$ 15.00 PRICE
3.75
GA
MC 1X
GA0 4
ZDN1009 8901 W. SUNSET, HOLLYWOO
A16SEP8 FRI OCT 30, 1998 8:00
* * * * * *
SUPERSUCKERS
AT THE
WHISKY A GOGO

Who wants a shot?

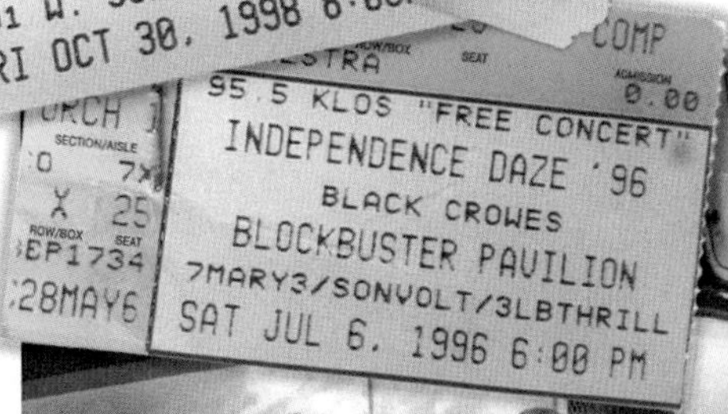
COMP
ADMISSION 0.00
ORCH
95.5 KLOS "FREE CONCERT"
INDEPENDENCE DAZE '96
BLACK CROWES
BLOCKBUSTER PAVILION
7MARY3/SONVOLT/3LBTHRILL
SAT JUL 6, 1996 6:00 PM
EP1734
28MAY6

NETH SCHWARTZ
GOLDEN GATE PARK
24 1995 at 12 NOON
with BAD RELIGION
Bill Graham Presents
Base Price 21.50
Service Fee 2.00
Total Price $23.50
$5 Per Order Fee
RAIN OR SHINE
ISSION 095480

Keep on rockin in a Free World, Baby

Ch
WHAT IS IT? CAUGHT IN A MOSH!

apter 7

"What is it? Caught in a Mosh!"

The Crazy World of Festival Shows, Sticking it to Ticketmaster When You Can, and Going Strong While Getting Kicked in the Face in a Mosh Pit

By now you all know I love music. I'll listen to anything once, and I'll go to any live show. And I go to a lot of them—like a shit ton of them—or at least I try to, probably about ten-twenty per year at this point in my life. I know some of you go to more, and let me just say—I'm super jealous. There's just no other way to put that. Good on you, and please let me know how they were. I'd love to hear all about them. What tours do I just have to see this year? Because I want to see them.

I'm shifting gears a bit this chapter and throwing out some 'metal advice' on festival shows. It's probably nothing you can't find on the Internet, but it's my book and my advice is based on my experiences and my love for music, so here you go:

First, let's get the obvious out of the way—festival shows are, usually, a great way to see a lot of bands at a great value. Instead of paying fifty dollars to see one or two bands, you pay a hundred dollars to see ten bands or more. They may not all be good bands, and they may not all be bands you even care to see. But for the most part, it's a good way to spend an afternoon and evening rocking out while enjoying a beer or two.

The first widely-known rock festival show was the Monterrey Pop Festival. The very same one my mom snuck out of the house to go see back when she was a young lass. I'm still jealous.

I know there were a few other music-type-shows that came along earlier than that—like the Newport Jazz Festival which started in 1954, and where a lot of great jazz, blues, and folk artists got their start.

There's actually a really good—but very weird—book about this festival, and a lot of other topics including religious cults, and the insanity that is Van Morrison—called *Astral Weeks*. There's some great music history in that book told by the people who were there, and I would recommend it if you have the time.

But the first *rock* festival is Monterrey Pop, followed by Woodstock, Altamont, and a whole host of others.

Back then, it seemed like a free-for-all. I never went, of course. I was too young. But I've seen enough coverage, documentaries, and books on all of the festivals I just mentioned, so I can make some assumptions.

Sure, some people did it the right way—bought tickets, paid for parking, lined up in a queue, and otherwise enjoyed the day responsibly. Then there were others who just hitchhiked to the gig in a VW Bus, hopped the fence, begged for food, danced in a cow field for three days straight, and then hitchhiked home.

Looking at you, Hippie Mom!

To be honest, I probably would've been the latter as well. Stick it to the man!

These days, 'the man' runs everything. It's all corporate—one giant music machine, and they're out to take your cash.

The Mayhem Festival sponsored by Rock Star Energy Drink.

Warped Tour sponsored by Vans.

Lollapalooza sponsored by C3.

What in the actual fuck is a C3?

Ok, I just looked it up, C3 is an AI cyber software company and they do some pretty cool shit, with people who are way smarter than me, and they sponsor a great rock festival, so now they are my favorite AI cyber software company ever!

Anyway, the festival shows have become ways for corporations to drive people to their products in the hopes of recouping their investment and making money.

Most of the festival shows I've gone to in the last ten-twenty years even have booths selling products that have nothing to do with the show you are seeing!

Want to buy a purse? Or some perfume? Or a new watch? There's a booth for that.

Want to give blood or register your DNA for a good cause (which I've done)? There's a booth for that.

Would you like sautéed beef short ribs with a marmalade demi glaze in a red wine reduction sauce, and a side of kale and farro? Yes, there's a fucking booth for that too!

And why? Because the corporations, and the sponsors, get to make more money.

There is an argument to be made for the fact that part of the reason this is all happening is due to baby boomers' demand and their spending influence on the Rock n Roll economy.

I'm not going to digress into an economic treatise on the value of the dollar and the changing taste in food consumption. I simply mention it here, because there is an argument that says it's the boomers allowing for all this corporate influence.

Baby boomers used to be the riff raff of the Rock n Roll world. Now they want luxury and accommodations, and they will price the new generations out of the Rock n Roll market to do so if they can.

Don't want to pay three hundred fifty dollars to see the latest rendition of the final Eagles tour? "That's okay, I can afford it," said the boomer, "and I'll go to the show. And you Millennials can watch it on HBO, or AXS TV, or Hulu, in a few months. Thanks, and have a nice day."

But do not despair, young Rock n Roller! There are plenty of shows where you still get in for a reasonably low price and still see a lot of great bands, even if that means you have to sit on the lawn. That's okay, you're in the building. You're rocking out, and you'll have a great story to tell for your book in twenty-thirty years. Rock on.

So, I wanted to write down some quick tips and thoughts on seeing festival shows these days. I'm sure I missed a few important things, but these are based on my experiences. Let me know what experiences you have, and the advice you'd give.

"Smoke on the Water"

Let's start with the most obvious one—HYDRATE!

Smoke your cigarettes, your cigars, your weed, whatever you want to smoke, but for god's sake, please hydrate.

Please, please, please, don't ever be that guy or gal that has to get carried out on a stretcher because you've been doing nothing but pounding beers all day in the hot sun while dancing and slamming and mosh pitting.

We've all seen that, and it's just no good.

It may be really cool to 'go big' like that for a while, but that's not the way your body was designed, and you need to take good care of it during the day so you can enjoy the entire show!

This should be blatantly obvious to any level-headed Rock n Roll show-goer and yet, at almost every festival show you go to, there's always that one person. Or probably more than one.

Imagine being the biggest fan of Pantera in the history of the world and going to see them at Ozz Fest. You are so psyched. You know every riff. You know every lyric. You can't wait to fist pump, throw your metal horns in the air, get in the pit, or otherwise dance around like a Whirling Dervish.

But your douchebag boyfriend decides to pound way too many overpriced Jack and Cokes during the opening band, Korn, and passes out on the grass before Pantera goes on.

Fucking Korn.

So now, you have to leave the show and look after his sorry ass, so he doesn't asphyxiate on his own Jack-flavored vomit sauce, and you miss the band you came to see.

Don't be that guy, please.

Yes, you can (and maybe you should) leave him behind in the medical tent, go back on Tinder, or call a divorce lawyer. It is Pantera, after all, and after this latest episode with your douchebag boyfriend, you are nothing short of "Fucking Hostile" (See what I did there?). But you're not that person—you're better than that, and now you have to go take care of his stupid ass and miss your favorite band and hold it over his head for the remainder of your natural born lives. Stupid boyfriend.

And people, if you're reading this book, and if I don't see a band performing locally soon called Jack Flavored Vomit Sauce, I'm going to be extremely disappointed.

"And You Put in Your Earplugs, Put on Your Eye Shades"

I wear earplugs to every show.

There, I said it.

Doesn't matter if I'm in the front row, the seats, or the grass.

I know that makes me uncool to some of you, and I don't fucking care.

Honestly, I'm not even sure why this is a 'thing' in the world of Rock n Roll.

Some people hate those of us that wear earplugs—calling us sell-outs, laughing at us, even taking pictures for their social media accounts and calling us "Pussies!" All of which has happened to me, by the way. Don't care.

And then there are those of us who look at people in the front row without earplugs and just shake our heads in disbelief.

Well, you know what side I stand on.

I'll be honest, for my first forty or fifty shows, I didn't wear earplugs either. I was a product of the 'fuck you, old man' generation in that regard. Look at the silly old people!

One show changed that for me forever.

Guns N' Roses is one of the best live shows I've ever seen. I described them a bit in an earlier chapter, but as I'm writing this book, I've seen them eleven or twelve times, with all variations of back-up band members—including the original lineup, and they've never disappointed. Not once.

On July 25, 1991, GNR played the Pacific Amphitheatre—an outdoor arena venue in Costa Mesa, CA.

I don't know if it was for this show specifically, or if it was part of their natural set-up, but the Pacific Amphitheater had a row of amps that extended out into the crowd, on both sides, for those of us lucky enough to sit close to the stage. So, you were essentially surrounded by a U-shape of amps delivering the heart-pounding music.

That night, I had pretty good seats towards the front—maybe twentieth row—and I sat about three seats in from the far-left aisle, so that I was looking at the right side of all the "Gunners" for the whole show.

Holy shit, did they rock that night. All their hits, half of *Appetite for Destruction*. A lot off the *Use Your Illusion* discs. And just some fun stuff to boot.

But it was loud!

And it was pounding in my left ear all show long.

Driving home, I couldn't hear a damn thing. But I was amped on adrenaline and I didn't care.

Next day, same thing.

Huh, usually after a good night's sleep and a ton of water (see Hydrate above!) this starts to go away, and my hearing returns back to normal. The hearing I needed in order to take food orders at the restaurants I worked at.

Second day after the show, same thing.

Oh, shit. This wasn't good. It's never taken this long to heal. I must've done some wicked stupid damage to my eardrums—or at least the one on my left side.

Third day, nope. No change.

Now, I'm freaking out.

Over the years, you read about legendary Rock n Rollers like Roger Daltrey or Pete Townsend or Bob Seger who have tinnitus, or some other really bad hearing problem—and it makes it hard from them to do the thing they love the most. To do the thing we love them to do the most.

"Later in the evening as you lie awake in bed
With the echoes from the amplifiers ringin' in your head
You smoke the day's last cigarette, remembering what she said."

Shit. I was heading in this direction and it was freaking me out.

Right then and there, I made a vow that I would forever wear ear plugs to every show I ever went to ever again. And to this day, I've never broken it.

Little club shows. Outdoor summer shows in the town square. Massive arena rock. Even festivals. I wear them all the time. And I'm so scared now, that I bring an extra pair—in case I drop the original ones when I take them out between sets. Or when that douchebag boyfriend who didn't hydrate slams into me in the pit and they fall out. Jerk.

On the fourth day, I woke up, and could hear normally. I was relieved.

I'm not sure what the long-term effect of that show will be. I'm coming up on thirty years since I went to that show.

And this may be the time in my life where my hearing will naturally start to disappear anyway. But I'm sure that night didn't help. I'm sure it might accelerate whatever issues are coming my way. And I know there are all sorts of cool new technology to help with that should it happen.

I just hope it doesn't. I hope my stupidity at that one show doesn't ruin the chances of me seeing additional shows going forward. We shall see.

But damn, it was a really good show!

"Caught in a Mosh"

Ah, the mosh pit. My Garden of Eden. My Shang-Ri-La. The place I hope they scatter my ashes when I die. Just a heavenly wonder of Rock n Roll aggression.

Aside from the obvious fun of slamming full speed into another human being while listening to your favorite bands, one of the reasons I love the pit is because there are rules.

In fact, there are more than rules; there is etiquette.

The same group of people that would probably fight each other in the parking lot over the last half can of "Natty Boh" beer, will go out of the way to make sure you are safe and taken care of in the pit. I fucking love that.

Here a few of the etiquettes I've picked up over the years.

1. The pit usually goes in one direction. Don't be the person going in through the out door.
2. Don't go for the face or man-parts (or lady parts for that matter). Don't flail your arms and legs around so someone gets really fucked up.
3. If someone falls, pick them up *immediately* so they don't get trampled and security has to stop the show.
4. If there are women or kids in the pit, it's ok to slam them a little gentler. I can hear some of you screaming about this point, but the fact is that women's bodies are just not designed as strong as men's and if a full-grown man

slams into a full-grown woman, it can do some lasting damage. Don't like this? Sorry, blame Charles Darwin. And kids are the future of the pit, so treat them well and let them lead the way. Show them all the beauty they possess inside. Give them a sense of pride. Dammit, Whitney, you're haunting me!

5. If someone is hurt, staggering, super-drunk, super-stoned, or laying on the ground bleeding, get them out of the pit as fast as you can and resume your holy metal pit slamming.
6. Hydrate! Take a break for half a song, have a soda, then get back in. It's okay—you're not a pussy.

Following a few of these basic rules ensures that the pit can continue for the entire show, that you, me, and they can have a good time, and that no one goes home with permanent damage—or dead.

And if you find my earplugs, please give them back to me!

"Let's Go Surfing Now, Everybody's Learning How"

Quick side note about stage diving and crowd surfing.

Both can be a lot of fun—if you do them right.

If you're lucky enough to hop on stage and jump off it before security catches you, please don't aim for the lightest, smallest, thinnest, most fragile person that you see.

Remember, the baby boomers now have all the money and usually sit in the front few rows with their kids or even their grandkids.

If you were to jump towards them, you're going to do some serious damage. Then all the other baby boomers in that section will kick your ass. And frankly, I will join them.

So, find a good spot—a spot of your peers, if you will. And before you jump, look at the people you're about to jump on and make sure they know you're coming. Then go have fun.

Crowd surfing is wicked fun. You have zero control and

you're just floating atop people's heads while listening to music. Talk about heaven! But a few rules apply here too.

Someone may drop you! They can't lift all two hundred pounds of your bony-ass body, so they simply let go and you crash down to the cement floor. So always protect your head, and be ready for this to happen at any moment.

See the rule above about flailing your arms and legs. People are doing you a service by moving your body over their head. Don't shit on them by waving your arms and banging their head's around. If you do, see Rule 1, and prepare to hit that concrete.

And if you see a woman crowd surfing, please don't be an asshole and start grabbing her in places you wouldn't want your mom or sister or daughter to be grabbed. I've seen this so much and it kills me. It's disgusting. Don't be that person ever. And tell your drunk friend to stop doing it too. Not cool. Full stop.

"And the Band Played On"

There are a few other fun things about festival shows that I wanted to put in this part of the chapter. Just some Rock n Roll knowledge I've accumulated over the years. You don't have to do all—or any—of these to have a good time, but they can enhance your festival going experience if you do them, at least in my opinion.

The headliners sell the show. They have the hits. They've earned the spots. But sometimes, the bands playing on the parking lot stage or side stage are way more fun.

It's the same theory I mentioned in an earlier chapter for bands like Pincushion Jones or Munkafust—they're trying harder. They want to have those hits. They want to earn the top spots. They want to headline the show.

I can't even count how many good bands I've seen on the second or third stage. Walking Papers. In This Moment. The Music. The Pretty Reckless. And so many more. Go spend the time and check them out. I promise you'll find a band or two that you like. Buy their CD after their set. Go meet them. Which brings me to...

Get their autograph! Who fucking cares? You're not a dork. You're not a loser. Buy their CD at the show, tell them you loved the set, and ask them to sign your CD cover.

At a lot of these festival shows, the side bands have booths where you can come meet them after the gig. Do it.

It's silly. It's fun. And you leave with a really cool souvenir! And who knows, that band you saw in the parking lot this year, may be headlining next year, and you can turn to your new boyfriend (since you ditched the last one after Pantera), and say, "Yeah, I met those guys, they were totally cool."

Last thing about the bands: even the bad ones are worth checking out. I don't mean the ones that can't play well. They won't be on the tour to begin with. I mean the ones you don't like.

We all have those bands we cannot stand. I list my Top Five in the next chapter. But for almost every band on that list, I always go see them too. Maybe they can change my mind. Maybe they are a lot better live than they sound on the radio. Open yourself up to that possibility–there are quite a few bands that used to be on that list that no longer are, because I saw them live and said 'shit, those boys can play. I'll give them another chance.' And I'm glad I did.

If you have a chance to get to the front row, do it. Swap tickets. Fake a wristband. Lie, cheat, and steal your way down there if you have to. It's just fucking epic.

You're the first person in the whole arena to hear those notes. You can see the faces of your Rock n Roll heroes as they wail on their Les Paul Gold Top. You might even get a high-five, a guitar pick, or a drumstick! But it's a great vibe and great atmosphere down in the front. Something everyone should check out at least once in their lives. Pay the extra money for the ticket if you have to, or just go back to the lie, cheat, and steal method I described earlier.

You need beer. You need soda. You need water. And these days, thanks to the Internet, you know what songs the band is going to play. So, time your exodus wisely. Go take that piss. Get in the beer line again. Check out the overpriced t-shirts. Your favorite songs are coming soon. You have time. Go take care of business.

Please do not be on your phone the whole time while you're at a show. Put it the fuck away. Okay, take a video or two of your heroes playing that song you love and post it. But don't fucking check your phone every three minutes to find out what Aunt Sadie said about your new haircut, or what your ex-boyfriend said about the song. Just stop—put away the electronics, and deal with it later.

While you're at any show, crowd watching is just one of the best things they have to offer.

"Is that guy wearing an original Iron Maiden Fear of the Dark t-shirt from 1992? Well, fuck, he gets a high-five!"

"Did you see those two metal chicks and what they were barely wearing? God bless America!"

"Is that guy wearing a Styx shirt to a KISS concert? We seriously need to beat him in the parking lot later on tonight."

The point is, don't be so wrapped up in your own shit that you forget to see what else is happening. Crowd watching should be an Olympic sport. It's fun and gives you lots of great stories to tell your friends.

Finally, leaving the show: there are two schools of thought on this. Leave early and avoid the rush, or stay through the encore and hear all your favorite songs—since you know they are going to play them towards the end.

This is, once again, when I show my age. When I was younger, I would bring water bottles, food, footballs, frisbees, folding chairs, and anything else I could think of, so I could stay 'til the end of a show, sit in the parking lot so all the other losers could go home before me, and, if I'm being honest, to help me sober up.

These days, I want out of there. I want to go home, and I want to go bed. I know I know, not very metal of me. But the parking lots at some of these places I see shows at are so horrible that I just want to get out of there as early as I can.

Jiffy Lube Live in Bristow, VA, and The Rose Bowl and Irvine Meadows Amphitheater, in California, are three places I will leave early from every time for the rest of my life. Three of the worst parking lot situations you will ever find. Although, it's been years since I went to those places in California, so they could have changed. Who knows? The Forum in L.A. with its multiple exit points, and any place near a Metro station in D.C.—The Capitol One Arena, DAR Constitution Hall—are some of the better ones.

But if I've seen Def Leppard multiple times, and I know "Photograph" is going to be the last song they play, then it's time for me to go. I've had a great night of rocking and now Daddy just wants his pjs, some Pepto, and his pillow. Rock on.

Chapter 7.1

"Money For Nothing"

I hate Ticketmaster, Live Nation, and all those other corporate behemoths that charge me a fucking "service fee" to go have a good time at a concert. Fuck you and your fee-based bullshit. What service am I paying for? Printing out a one-inch by three-inch piece of paper with writing on it and sticking it in an envelope—which you have a robot do for you anyway? Or these days, sending me an email with my ticket attached as a jpg?

A .jpg costs me $14 fucking dollars?

If you were handing me my ticket with one hand, and giving me a hand job with the other, fine, you can keep your damn service fee—and I might even sincerely thank you, but otherwise, fuck off. Damn corporate Rock n Roll assholes.

Okay, I feel better, thank you.

We all know there isn't much we can do about this. It's just something that we now 'accept' as part of the concert-going experience. And it sucks. But we still keep going to shows, so we'll still keep paying those fees.

Many of you know that bands like Pearl Jam took this fight to a whole new level in the '90s, even as much as testifying before the U.S. Congress about the monopolistic practices of companies like Ticketmaster.

Pearl Jam testified that they would play a venue and be forced to use Ticketmaster as the ticket service provider for that venue, and that Ticketmaster could charge whatever "service fee" they wanted, no matter what cost the band wanted to charge their fans.

When they tried to play another venue, they found out that Ticketmaster had an agreement with that venue as well.

No matter where they went, bands like Pearl Jam were forced to use this system, or they wouldn't be allowed to play in that arena for their fans.

There were simply not a lot of other options.

Pearl Jam did a tour in the '90s where they only played arenas that had nothing to do with Ticketmaster. I don't think it was very successful, but I love them for trying.

In July of 1994, bassist Jeff Ament and guitarist Stone Gossard, went to Capitol Hill, dressed to the nines—ahem, as only grunge rock legends could dress—and testified about their experiences with being forced to use this process.

And wouldn't you know it, but Congress was so moved—so overwhelmed with this new knowledge, and so thankful that these young lads took the time to exercise their constitutional rights to air their grievances and petition their elected representatives, that Congress decided to tear down the Ticketmaster monopoly and free millions of fans around the country from the tyranny of the so-called fucking service fee!

Yeah, okay. Not really.

As usual, the assholes in Congress were more concerned about the monthly PAC money given to them by Ticketmaster's public affairs team over the reality that this is the utter fucking definition of a monopoly, and let Ticketmaster have their way and continue along with their draconian practices.

Fuck.

Thank you for trying Pearl Jam, and other bands that made the effort. You don't know how much that meant to a music nerd like me.

But, guess what music fans—there are ways around it. It's illegal in most states. But it's fun as hell. And it's called scalping.

I have entered so many shows for free. For five dollars. For ten dollars. For the price of buying someone a beer. I've even managed to get a date out of it! Why? All because I've shown up and tried. Screw Ticketmaster and their fee-based bullshit. You want to go see a show? Go see a goddam show.

Look, like I said—this is illegal in many states. And most venues have security and local rent-a-cops scouring the area for just this sort of behavior. I'm sure the fine isn't that steep, but I don't know for real, and I'm not offering to pay it if you get caught—so don't listen to me if you don't want to. If you think you're going to get in trouble, then don't do it.

I'm sure the lawyers for this publishing company are very happy I said that. Here you go, lawyers, does this help?

"We, the publishers of this book, do not condone any such unlawful behavior heretofore and forthwith regarding the issue of scalping."

There you have it.

But whatever.

As I said, you want to go see a show, go see a show. Here's some ideas on how you can get it done:

There is always an extra ticket. The show could be sold out in world-record-time, which leaves you bummed out. You're not getting in. Life is over. Goodbye, cruel world.

Oh, for fuck's sake, suck it up, snowflake.

Go to the show. Find a place to park. Uber in. Whatever. Just go.

Walk through the parking lot for a while. Stick one finger in the air but keep it close to your body as if you're holding the #1 on your chest.

Be friendly and nod to the folks who are tailgating or parking or just hanging out and chilling. Right when you get near them, say something like "looking for one," or "need one ticket" or "got one to sell?" or something like that.

Not too loud but loud enough that they can hear you.

If that doesn't work, head toward the gates. But be careful.

This is where security is hanging out. So, what I do is I look like I'm waiting for my friend. I check my watch. I check my phone. I've even pretended to be on the phone when I saw security headed in my general direction.

"Yeah man, where are you? You said to meet you out front. I've been standing here, asshole."

My phone: "If you'd like to make another call, check the number, hang up, and dial again."

"Dude, I don't care if she wants to blow you in the parking lot. Ozzy is on in ten minutes. Get over here, or you're buying the first round of beer!"

"Thank you for calling Bank of America. Goodbye."

And they were none the wiser.

After they go away, stick that one finger up and whisper the magic words. "Looking for one, looking for one" is always my favorite.

Someone always has an extra ticket to sell. Someone told their buddy to get a ticket, and swore they would go, and then backed out for some reason—leaving his 'former friend' stuck with the ticket and a big debt! Or maybe it's not that evil. Maybe someone got sick, had to go out of town, or take care of a relative. It happens. But there is *always* an extra ticket.

Now the person selling that ticket, if they're smart, knows they are not going to get face value for it, although they will try. They paid seventy-five bucks for that ticket, including all the goddam service fees, and they would like all their money back—but deep down, they just want to make something off of it so it's not a total, complete loss.

Offer them ten bucks.

If they tell you to fuck off and pay them the full seventy-five, I always politely, and with a smile, say "no thank you, I just want to sit in the grass and enjoy the show, but good luck man, and have a great time."

Then the negotiation begins.

"Come on man, give me at least fifty."

"I'm good bud, I really didn't want to go higher than fifteen, so I'll find someone else or just head home if I need to, but really, good luck—I saw some guys over there looking as well."

"Fuck, how about at least twenty then?"

"Sold! Thanks for the ticket, have a nice day!"

He feels like he got you up ten from your original price, and makes a little cash, even though he probably still hates the friend that ditched him. And you just got a brand spanking new ticket to see Breaking Benjamin for the low, low, price of twenty American dollars.

And guess what? No fucking service fees.

Bam.

Don't be a dick—have your cash ready before they change their mind, and be fully prepared in your head to leave the venue and go home if it doesn't work (or if security makes you), and I promise you, you'll succeed at this 90% of the time or better.

I've seen at least fifty shows this way over the years. I used to live right near Jiffy Lube Live in Bristow, VA—the one with the seriously awful parking lot. I would head home from work on a Tuesday night and hear on the radio that Rush, Tom Petty, Shinedown, or Linkin Park were playing tonight and "hey music fan, come on down".

So, I did what they asked: I came on down.

I parked the car—for free. Jiffy Lube has the price of parking in with their tickets. Walked the lot or hung out by the front gates, stuck my #1 in the air by my chest and said the magic words, and got a ticket to all those shows for as little as five dollars.

Then, of course I left early and got in my pjs, but fuck it—I'm old!

Chapter 7.2

"Ain't That a Kick in Head"

I have to end this story with what may have been my last adventure in the mosh pit ever. I got kicked in the face. Hard. And I paid a ridiculous sum of money to enjoy that "privilege" as well.

Because the music industry isn't so much of an industry anymore—no CD release parties, no music stores, no corporate machine apparatus behind the bands—a lot of times bands find new and unique ways to make money.

One of these ways is the overpriced meet-and-greet. You can pay X amount of dollars, stand in line and meet your heroes, and then get good seats to the concert and have a unique experience that those dorks in the grass, like me, just won't understand.

I did this once. And I'll never do it again.

A buddy of mine really liked the band Disturbed. Like, a lot. I was tepid on them. They have some really good songs, and some really just-okay songs, and everything in between. A good solid live band though, I will say, and David Draiman's voice is pretty damn amazing.

A few years ago, the lads from Disturbed were coming through town and my buddy convinced me to do the overpriced meet-and-greet. "Okay, fine—let's try this," I said, and forked over two-hundred fifty dollars for the experience.

We got there way early—because we were told to get their way early, as part of the experience.

We queued up with about five hundred other mega-Disturbed fans in the hot sun, because this was going to be an experience!

And from six-seven pm, about an hour before the opening band came on, the line started to move. Some folks got giddy. I was just curious.

We wound around behind the stage and into the back area where the roadies bring gear in and out. We headed toward some cool little hangout area, and wound up and down some stairs.

Then, magically, we turn the corner and there were the boys from Disturbed, dressed to the 9's in their metal fineness.

"Wow, this line is moving rather swiftly," I remember thinking.

Pretty soon, we were next to meet them. Some roadie grabbed me by the shoulder and pushed me forward. I shook each of the guy's hands, took a photo, and was once again gently pushed off the stage. They handed us a 'goodie bag' filled with some pretty decent Disturbed swag and off we went back to the pit to await the show.

Honestly, it took me longer to insert the photo you see at the end of this chapter.

Bing. Bam. Boom. Two-hundred fifty dollars.

So, let's do a little math. $250 each x 500 people in line = $125,000. 125k x 50 shows on the tour = $6,250,000.

The band made six million fucking dollars for doing one hour of handshakes in fifty cities on a tour. Would you do that? Uh, fuck yeah you would. That's nuts. Insane. Crazy.

But you know what? Good for them. And all the other rockers who are doing this. Just like the rest of us, they have to adapt to the times, and they found a way to do it that makes a lot of people very happy and gives them memories for life.

As I'm writing this chapter, the latest Guns N Roses tour was just announced. I just looked at tickets for their show at Nats Park in DC in July 2020. You can get this same sort of package—3rd row seats, a meet-and-greet with the boys, a bag of cool swag, and a memory to last a lifetime.... for nine-hundred dollars each.

Doing the same math, that's $22.5 million dollars over fifty dates. Holy shit.

Seriously, why don't rock bands turn into Pete Rose, plop themselves down in a mall somewhere, and charge fifty dollars for an autograph and a hundred for a photo. It's probably heading in that direction. Good luck, Gunners.

So, after this overpriced meet-and-greet, my buddy and I headed to the pit like I said. It was cool to be down there as always. The energy is just so fucking great.

We sorta stayed towards the back of the pit—close enough to the action, but far enough away from the madness. I guess we were maturing as Rock n Roll fans.

But there's one Disturbed song I fucking love. One that's always on my iPod at the gym. One that gets me cranked up. "Inside the Fire" is just a monster song. This, along with "Ten Thousand Fists" are probably their best songs, in my opinion, and I just love these songs so much.

"Devin, Won't go to heaven
She's just another lost soul, about to be mine again
Leave her, we will receive her
It is beyond your control; will you ever meet again."

This song has that great intro, a great build up, excellent guitars, and it just fucking rocks.

So, when this song started, I looked to my buddy, handed him my old-man glasses and bag of overpriced Disturbed swag, and said 'fuck it, I'm going in.'

I ran into the mosh pit at full speed. I bounced into a few surly motherfuckers, and started going in a circle—the right way, not the wrong way—following the rules of mosh pit etiquette.

I got halfway around my first circle. Someone pushed me in the back, and I fell forward. At the same time, the guy in front of me started flailing his arms and feet. As I went down, his foot came up, and clocked me right in the fucking face. Jean Claude Van Damme from the movie Kickboxing couldn't have done it any better. Epic strike.

My head snapped back and hit the ground hard. There may have been a second or two I didn't remember as I was counting the Tweety-Birds circling around my head.I remember getting up off the ground and onto all fours.

Here I am, on all fours in the middle of a mosh pit that's still going strong while a band I dig is playing my favorite song. And I can barely remember my name.

Luckily, thanks to mosh pit etiquette, some dude recognized the danger to me, and my fellow moshers. He picked me under my arms, asked me if I was okay, escorted me to the edge of the circle, and released me before heading back into the swirling mess behind me.

I stumbled back over to my buddy who handed me my glasses and said, "you're a fucking idiot" while laughing and also holding me up.

I remember throwing up some metal horns at the end of that song. We went home soon after. That shit hurt for days. Not just my face, but the fact that I paid two-hundred fifty dollars to enjoy that face kick. I chose to do that. I wanted to do that. Also, it's probably my last time in a mosh pit since I don't seem to be doing it right anymore.

Anybody want to buy a bag of overpriced Disturbed swag?

I'll sell it cheap.

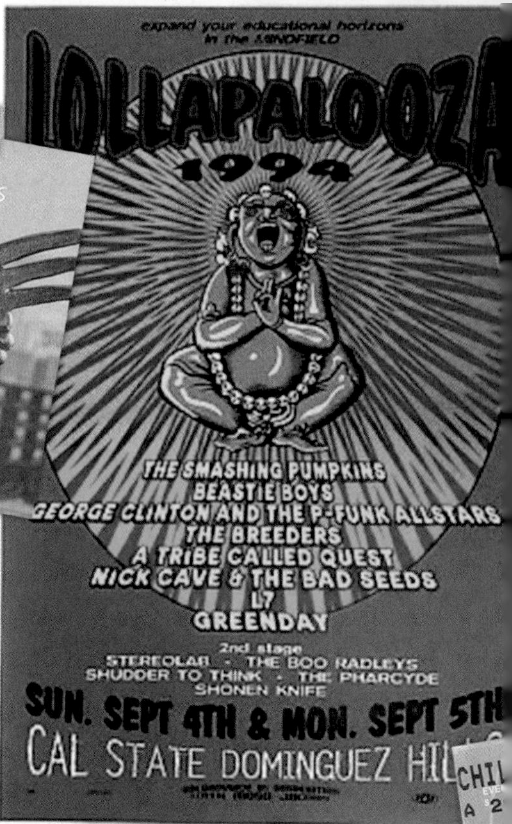

Wear your damn ear plugs! Trust me

101 CHILI COOK-OFF '07
PRESENTED BY
NKF AND BUD LIGHT
IN OR SHINE/GATES @11AM
11TH & NEW YORK AVE NW
SAT MAY 12, 2007 11AM
GENERALADMISSION
GAX2 GA6 46 20.00

V0703 GA GA51153 C 0.00
GENERAL ADMISSN +FCSURG
GOLDENVOICE / KROQ
VANS WARPED TOUR 97
AT THE
OLYMPIC VELODROME
CAL STATE DOMINGUEZ HILLS
THU JUL 3, 1997 12 NOON

Inside the Fire rocks
but, my face
still hurts

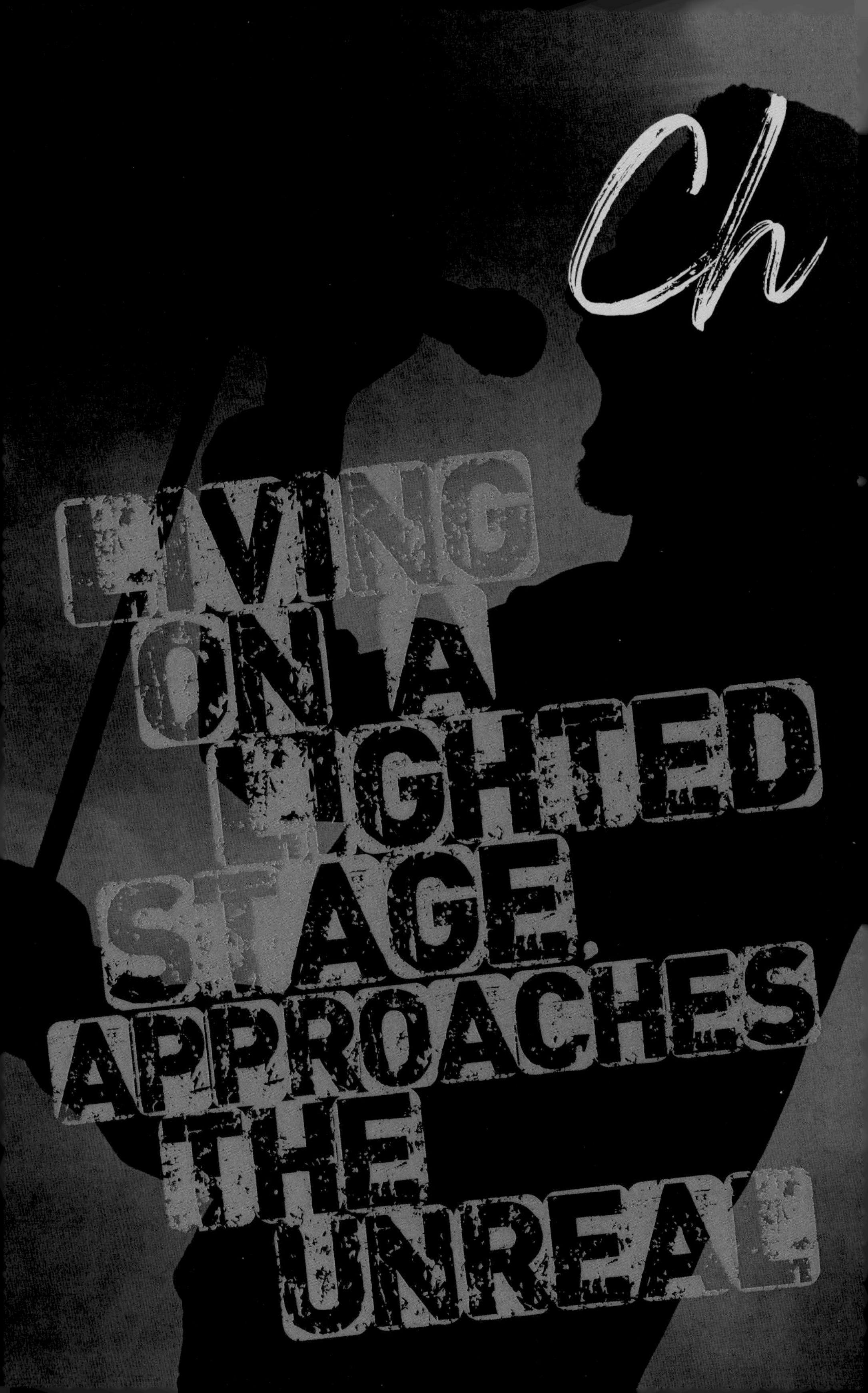

Ch
LIVING ON A LIGHTED STAGE APPROACHES THE UNREAL

apter 8

"Living on a Lighted Stage, Approaches the Unreal"

The List Chapter! From the Rainbow to the Jiff, an Ode to All the Great Places I've Enjoyed Music in my Life

Ok, let's debate.

We all love lists. We rarely agree with them. But we love them. They are great for office water cooler conversation. Morning DJs use them for endless hours of chitchat. And thanks to the Internet, everyone has a voice—for good or for bad—and can weigh in on what they think as well.

That's what I want to happen here. This chapter is all about my favorite things. My favorite bands, my favorite songs, and my favorite places to see a show (and some not-so-great bands, songs, and places as well).

But what do *you* think? I really want to know. Tweet us at @AllTheCoolBands and we'll have that debate. I guarantee I'll respond to as many as I can!

"Hey Ken, how could you forget to put ________ on the list of Top 5 drummer, you fucking asshole."

"Crap, Todd, you're right, that's a great point."

"Hey Ken, you put that video on your Top 5 list? You know it's considered one of the worst videos of all time, right?"

"Shit, Craig, we're just gonna have to agree to disagree on that one."

And so on.
Let's do this.

Top 5 Favorite Bands of All Time

1. Led Zeppelin
2. Def Leppard
3. Guns N Roses
4. AC/DC
5. Pearl Jam

I talk a lot in this book about Def Leppard. And they are truly the band that got me into Rock n Roll like no other band ever did. But Led Zeppelin is just the best. Yes, even better than my boys from Sheffield. I'm sure they would agree with this too. The quality of the music is superior, and they are truly the legends they deserve to be. Def Leppard and GNR produced some of best music ever made. AC/DC is just too much fun not to be on the list. And Pearl Jam was by far the best band to come out of the 'grunge era,' and are still making great music to this day.

Top 5 LEAST Favorite Bands of All Time

1. Depeche Mode
2. The Cure
3. 311
4. Stain'd
5. Creed

God, I hate these bands. I never got into Creed or Stain'd, but everything I heard was just not good to my ears. 311's music just simply rubs me the wrong way, and I never found the right way. I did have a goth phase in college, and even then, still couldn't listen to The Cure—that's how much I hated their music. And "Depressed Mode" just plain fucking sucks. When every instrument is played through a keyboard, you can suck my ass. How the Rock n Roll Hall of Fame elected them in 2020 is a travesty, but we'll get to the Rock Hall in a bit. In short, they suck.

And before you blast me, yes—I've actually seen Creed, Stain'd, and 311 in concert. 311 twice! I figured I would give them all a chance to change my mind, a chance to impress me, and a chance to show me what they could do. I wasn't impressed. Some bands do change my mind after a live show—I was never a huge fan of Shinedown until I saw them live, but they put on a damn good show. Some bands make me go the other direction. But these three I just couldn't get into.

And Depressed Mode still sucks ass.

Top 5 Bands I've Seen the Most

1. The Supersuckers—26 times
2. Def Leppard—16 times
3. Oingo Boingo—13 times
4. Guns N Roses—11 times
5. Skid Row—10 times

These numbers are at the time I'm writing this book. I have tickets to Def Leppard this summer and I'm debating buying a ticket for Guns N Roses too, so these numbers will change. Anyway, onward. This list is a little bit of vanity and a little bit of 'why the fuck would you spend so much money on all these shows' sorta thing. I do go to a lot of shows, and I love seeing new bands, but I love my old bands too. They are my comfort food, and my happy place. When I'm sad and blue, or when I just want to rock, I put these bands on, and all is well.

I also laugh at how much I've spent seeing these five bands alone. Seventy-six times! Seventy-six evenings of kick ass Rock n Roll. However, whenever I look at my checkbook and wonder why it's so low, I just look over to my stack of tickets, and say, 'oh, that's why!'

Who have you seen the most?

Top 5 Greatest Shows I've Seen in My Life

1. Guns N Roses–L.A. Forum–their first ever headlining tour
2. Oingo Boingo–Irvine Meadows Amphitheatre–Halloween
3. AC/DC–Long Beach Arena
4. Tom Petty–Jiffy Lube Live
5. Soundgarden & The Pixies–DAR Constitution Hall / Def Leppard–In The Round In Your Face

I will never forget that GNR show as long as I live. Thanks to some friends in the entertainment industry–oddly, not 'friends of Red Schwartz' this time–we had eighth row center seats to the first ever GNR headline tour ever. They were on top of their game, and blew the roof off the place. And I'll never forget Axl coming to the microphone and saying "hey L.A., every show we've ever done up to this point has been a warmup for tonight, and every show we do after tonight just won't mean as much. Thank you from the bottom of our hearts" before launching into "It's So Easy." It was some heartfelt goodness from Axl–who was known to spew bluster, and it just meant so much. I've already talked about Boingo shows and how good they were. AC/DC used cannons in their set during "For Those About to Rock"–FIRE! We salute you! If you can't get excited about cannons, what the fuck is wrong with you? Tom Petty was a hit machine–I can't recall another show where I knew every lyric to every song played. Literally every, single, one. Soundgarden and the Pixies lit up this small, four thousand-person arena in D.C. and sounded so good, and the Sheffield boys set world records for the In The Round tour. There are so many more I want to add to this list, but here it is.

Top 5 Least Favorite Shows of All Time

1. Kings of Leon–Jiffy Lube Live
2. The White Stripes–El Rey Theatre, L.A.
3. Styx–Jiffy Lube Live
4. Swervedriver–Dragonfly, L.A.
5. Fuel–Fishhead Cantina, Maryland

I do like these bands. I have many CD's by each of them. But, for one reason or another, these shows were just not that great. The Kings of Leon are a solid band with some really good music, but that night, they had zero energy. They didn't interact with the crowd; they played their songs and went home. I could have stayed home and put their CD on in my living room and had the same experience. Maybe they were sick? Who knows? I friggin' love me some Jack White and the White Stripes, but when you see just a guitar and drummer play for two hours, you're missing half the sound of the songs. Where's the bass? Where's the bottom? Where's the rhythm? It didn't work. Styx are legends, but I think there was one original member playing that night, and it just wasn't the same. And the last two were due to technical issues. Swervedriver was having guitar troubles, and they were a swirly guitar wah wah pedal type of band, so they sounded nothing like themselves. Fuel tried to play some local beer bar near the Baltimore airport, who weren't ready to have a legit band play there. They couldn't make the equipment work, played three-four acoustic songs, including two Zeppelin covers, and then we all went home. I'll give Fuel credit–they wanted to interact with the fans at a bar they all liked going to, but it just came off as one big ball of blah.

p 5 Bands I Wish I Saw

1. Nirvana
2. Prince
3. David Bowie
4. Scorpions
5. UFO

Say what you will about Nirvana—they were an obvious force in the music industry for reasons I don't need to explain here. I had a chance to see them, but my buddy convinced me to come party with him in Arizona, and I swore I would "go see Nirvana the next time they toured." Well, oops. That didn't happen, but I wish I saw them. I just flat out missed Prince, David Bowie, and the Scorpions. I would have loved to see Prince, just for the entertainment value and booty-shaking songs. Bowie is the king! And the Scorpions are in their 'sixth year' of their farewell tour as I write this, so maybe I'll get a chance to check them out after all. I was never a huge UFO fan until I started listening to Eddie Trunk from Sirius XM and "That Metal Show" fame. I checked them out, now love them, and I wish I saw them live.

Quick side note—I'm sure some of you are wondering why groups like Led Zeppelin or The Beatles aren't on here. I tried to not add bands that came and went before I was around. That just didn't seem fair. Zeppelin broke up when I was nine. The Beatles, when I was negative one. That said, I did see Jimmy Page and The Black Crowes do two hours of Zeppelin at the Greek Theatre in L.A., and I have seen Paul McCartney do a lot of Beatles songs. Since I'm not from that era, that's good enough for me.

Top 5 Most Underrated Bands of All Time

1. Triumph
2. ELO
3. UFO
4. Supersuckers
5. Thin Lizzy

Why aren't these bands bigger? Why do we not revere them like we do The Stones or Ozzy? I don't know. Someone please explain it to me. Triumph is the best three-piece rock band to ever come out of Canada, after those guys who wrote that song about Mark Twain's book, Tom Sawyer. They are so good! You might say that ELO has received a lot of attention in the last twenty years as being one of the best live acts of all time, and I may not be able to argue that point, but they just don't seem to get the respect they're due. I've talked about UFO and the Supersuckers before, and Thin Lizzy is loved by rockers old and young—just a really fucking great band.

Top 5 Bands That Are Huge, and I Should Probably Love Them More But I Just Don't

1. U2
2. Dave Matthews Band
3. Bruce Springsteen
4. Bob Dylan
5. REM

This list was hard to write. These are all legends. And I've seen them all live, except Dylan. They've had historic careers, wrote some of the best songs ever made, and put on epic tours. But every time they come on the radio, I go to the next station. I'll put this all on my brain and me. Something inside my synapses isn't letting me appreciate these legends as much as I should. I've tried, but it ain't working. Got nothing but love and respect for who they are—but I'm gonna change the channel now, thank you.

Top 5 Best Places to See a Show

1. The Roxy, Troubadour, & L.A. Forum—L.A.
2. DAR Constitution Hall, 9:30 Club—D.C.
3. The Off-Ramp—Seattle
4. Casino Del Sol—Tucson
5. Merriweather Post, Jiffy Lube Live—D.C. Area

Ok, I cheated a bit on this list and put eight instead of five. I've been to so many places, it was hard to nail it down to just five. I grew up in a L.A. and was at all those places so many times for so many good shows. Great acoustics, great atmosphere, and a lot of fun was had every time I went. DAR and the legendary 9:30 Club are by far D.C.'s best places to see a show. Some huge acts play at these small places, and you can really connect to the music you love. The Off-Ramp was a legendary place where all the Seattle bands played. I saw The Gits play there one night, not long before tragedy befell the lead singer—but it was such a great place to bounce around and rock. Casino del Sol surprised me. I got off a plane one day, and my buddy handed me a free ticket to go see Velvet Revolver, so I went—and it was legendary. And pound for pound, both Jiffy Lube Live and its Maryland cousin, The Merriweather Post Amphitheater, are just fun places to see big acts with twenty-thirty thousand of your closest friends.

Top 5 Favorite Front Men

1. Axl Rose
2. Joe Elliott
3. Eddie Vedder
4. Brian Johnson
5. Danny Elfman

This list shouldn't surprise anyone who's gotten this far in the book. It goes hand in hand with my favorite bands. Who am I missing? Who are yours?

Top 5 Favorite Frontwomen

1. Pat Benatar
2. Sheryl Crow
3. Lzzy Hale
4. Cristina Adriana Chiara Scabbia
5. Taylor Momsen & Johnette Napolitano

Let's give it up for the ladies for a sec, shall we? I actually prefer female lead singers and have a CD in my car right now with twenty of my favorite female singers of all time—from Aretha, to Pat Benatar, to Taylor Dayne! Hey, don't judge—someday I'll be your shelter too. But these ladies just flat-out rock. Period. Full stop. And they deserved their own list. Pat and Sheryl are music icons, and put on some damn good shows. Halestorm blew me away live, and I've been in love with Lzzy Hale ever since. Like head over heels, as in girl—please call me.

If you don't know Lacuna Coil, go buy their albums right now and rock out to the amazing Cristina Scabbia. For being a former Cindy Lou Who, I gotta say that Taylor Momsen rocks The Pretty Reckless with her soulful bluesy voice and extremely tight outfits, and Johnette did the same with Concrete Blonde thirty years ago. Both wicked amazing bands.

Top 5 Best Guitarists of All Time

1. Jimi Hendrix
2. Jimmy Page
3. Eric Clapton
4. Eddie Van Halen
5. Slash

This was by far the hardest list to come up with, and usually the most-debated in all those water-cooler, morning-show places I was talking about earlier. There are literally hundreds of guitarists that could fill this list—Lindsay Buckingham, Neil Young, Paul McCartney, Phil Collen, Vivian Campbell, Angus Young, Yngwie Malmsteen, and Ritchie Blackmore. But there are so many more. I put my five favorites, and the one that sort of changed guitar music forever on top. But I'd really like to know what you think so tweet me at @AllTheCoolBands and we'll hash it out.

Top 5 Drummers of All Time

1. Neil Peart
2. John Bonham
3. Ginger Baker
4. Stewart Copeland
5. Matt Cameron & Gil Moore

Unlike the guitar list, this one is definitive and final. No opinions needed or wanted. Don't tweet me because you're wrong. Move on to the next list. Okay, not really—but these are my favorites and I dare you to try and knock one of them off my list. I go back and forth between Neil and Bonham all the time. I know Neil revered Bonham, so maybe Zep should be on top? But given Neil's passing, and his legendary list of songs, drum fills, and lyrics, I'm going to put him on top. Ginger Baker was a fucking whack-a-doodle, but he put all that energy into his skins, and it came out great. Some people love The Police, and some people hate them. But as amazing as Sting is, Copeland drove that band with his drumming. Matt Cameron is the force behind Soundgarden and lately, Pearl Jam—and is amazing live. And I snuck in Gil Moore, the drummer from Triumph, because I cannot listen to "Fight the Good Fight" and "Lay It On The Line" without some serious air drumming in my car or at the gym.

Top 5 Bassists of All Time

1. John Entwistle
2. Les Claypool
3. Geddy Lee
4. John Paul Jones
5. John Taylor and Steve Harris

I'll admit, I don't know the bass that well, so there could be some I'm missing here, but when I was putting this list together, these were the ones that popped into my head. The

Who, Zeppelin, and Rush need no explanation. Les Claypool from Primus did things with the bass that violated the laws of physics, much less the laws of music. That guy was a fucking nutter, but man could he play that thing. And he danced around the stage while doing it!

What a showman John Taylor was as the stud behind Duran Duran. If you listen to that group, they are all (mostly) very heavy bass-driven songs. The bass line for "Rio" alone earns him a spot on this list. Go listen to that song again and focus just on the bass. You'll see what I mean.

Steve Harris is in Iron Fucking Maiden. 'Nuff Said.

Top 5 Supergroups

1. Cream
2. Temple of the Dog
3. Travelling Wilburys
4. Neurotic Outsiders
5. The Down N Outz

Cream should really be on this list by itself. No one will ever touch them as best supergroup of all time. Ever. I love Temple of the Dog, but Cream blows them out of the water—and I guarantee Eddie Vedder would agree with this. Jack Bruce, Eric Clapton, and Ginger Baker at the height of their talent—in one group? Holy shit. They didn't last long, but what they gave us was legendary. Travelling Wilburys should probably be #2, but Temple of the Dog came out right when I needed them to in my life and they get the nod—but both groups are so much fun to listen to. The Neurotic Outsiders was a mix of Duran Duran, The Sex Pistols, Guns N Roses, and even Billy Idol! Their music is not for the faint of heart. Go put on the song "Nasty Ho" at your next family reunion, and see how fast you get taken out of the will. The Down N Outz is a Joe Elliot side project with some of his glam rock heroes that got him into music in the '70s. So, any bands that got Joe Elliott to make music is pretty okay by me.

Top 5 Rock Documentaries/Movies of All Time

1. *The Wall* and *Heavy Metal*
2. *Beware of Mister Baker*
3. *Rush: Time Stand Still*
4. *Maiden 666*
5. *All Things Must Pass* and *The Rainbow*

If I can't rock out to music live, I sure do love watching the history of it on my TV screen. *The Wall* and *Heavy Metal* are not only legendary, and filled with great music, but they are also the first two things I got stoned to, so they will always be #1 in my heart (but maybe not in my lungs). *Beware of Mister Baker* surprised me. I wasn't expecting much, and it blew me away. As I said earlier, this guy is a fucking nut, but one of the best drummers of all time. Go watch and find out why. The Rush documentary is a look at their forty year career, and it's pretty damn fantastic. Listening to Geddy Lee talk about how his mother accepted his musical career is just so heartwarming and funny, how can you not love that man. *Maiden 666* is hilarious, and the music is so timeless. *All Things Must Pass* is about Tower Records, and *The Rainbow* is about, well, The Rainbow Bar & Grill on Sunset Strip. Both are places I've spent a lot of time and money, and the history in these docs are fun to watch.

And don't think I forgot about *Spinal Tap*. It is, hands down, the one and only best Rock n Roll mock-umentary in the history of cinema, so no list is needed here. Hello Cleveland!

Top 5 Videos of All Time

1. Looks That Kill—Motley Crüe
2. Foolin'—Def Leppard
3. Even Flow—Pearl Jam
4. November Rain—Guns N Roses
5. Here I Go Again—Whitesnake

Wait, chicks dig metal? That's the lesson I took from the first two videos on this list, and oh yeah, they are great songs to boot. Even Flow was the anti-video. Just a great band rocking on stage, and Eddie jumping into the crowd from the rafters. November Rain is beautiful, and really, *really* fucking weird. There are still websites to this day dedicated to trying to describe what the hell is happening in this video, but its so fun and silly and stupid, how can it not make the list? Two words for Whitesnake–Tawny Kitaen. Yeah, you know what I mean....

Chapter 8.1

"Party in the U.S.A."

A Quick Nod to the Rock Hall, and Also Who the Fuck Decides These Things?

As I get to writing this part of this chapter, the Rock n Roll Hall of Fame in Cleveland, Ohio recently announced their list of inductees for 2020:

- The Doobie Brothers
- Whitney Houston
- Nine Inch Nails
- The Notorious BIG
- T-Rex
- Jon Landau
- Irving Azoff
- Depressed Mode

I would like to drive to Cleveland and meet the people who decided that Depeche Mode should be in the Rock n Roll Hall of Fame, and I literally would like to punch you in the nut sack (or lady nut sack). You fucking suck.

How does a band that can barely play anything other than a keyboard get into the Rock n Roll Hall of Fame before bands like Thin Lizzy, The MC-5, and Iron Fucking Maiden? Please explain this to me.

Okay, thanks for letting me rant a bit.

This year's class is, should we say, not exactly the biggest purveyors of Rock n Roll in Rock n Roll history. Remember when Biggie came out with that #1 rock song? All those Led Zeppelin covers that Depeche Mode did on stage? That huge metal hit Whitney Houston sang at the Super Bowl?

Yeah, me neither.

Super stoked for T-Rex, NIN, and The Doobies—they deserve it. Kudos to them. But to snub people like Lizzy, Judas Priest, and Pat Benatar is a huge horrible oversight—and one that I hope they correct soon.

But here's the truth: The Rock n Roll Hall of Fame is nothing more than a money-making venture—just like most everything else—and they want fans of *all* kinds of music to come visit them in Cleveland, Ohio.

And while I hate the fact that a so-called band like Depressed Mode has a space in those hallowed halls before the likes of metal gods Iron Maiden, it is what it is—and there isn't much we can do about it.

I went to the Hall of Fame around 2009. I drove from D.C. to Cleveland, which surprisingly isn't that far—only about six hours. I'm so happy I went, and I want to go back. Unless they ban me after reading this chapter, of course. In fact, I like it so much, I sent them some of my dad's stuff that I had boxed up in the attic. It was lots of music memorabilia about Tommy James, Dick Clark, life in the record business, photos, notes, etc. They have it all, and I hope they display it someday, if they haven't already. That would excite me to no end, seeing "Redz" in the Rock n Roll Hall of Fame.

I'm not saying this to curry favor with the Hall of Fame, but I highly encourage you to go check it out some day. You can get lost in those halls and relive all those great moments that made your life so special. Go see an Indians, Browns or Cavs game. Check out Lake Erie. It's a good, low-cost three or four-day weekend with the family to mid-America where the people are super-friendly, and the food is super-fried!

And when you go, ask them for the Iron Maiden display, just to make them squirm.

Man. this gu is SO crazy good!

Izzy ROCKS!

I am just
a cowboy...

THE CURE
LULLABY (OSCAR OZZ EDIT)

THE
GRIND

Best video ever?????

EVENT CODE
LOGE 5
SECTION/AISLE
UU 503
ROW/BOX SEAT
IRU0955
912FEB2

UU 503
ROW/BOX ADULT

COCA-COLA/AVALON BRING YO
S K I D R O W
RAIN OR SHINE
IRVINE MEADOWS AMPH.
ALT/FLT MAY CAUSE PSTPNM
SAT MAR 14, 1992 8:00 PM

Philip P Lynott

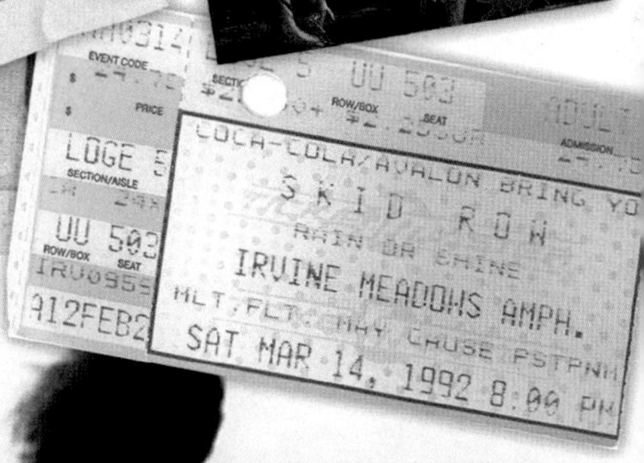

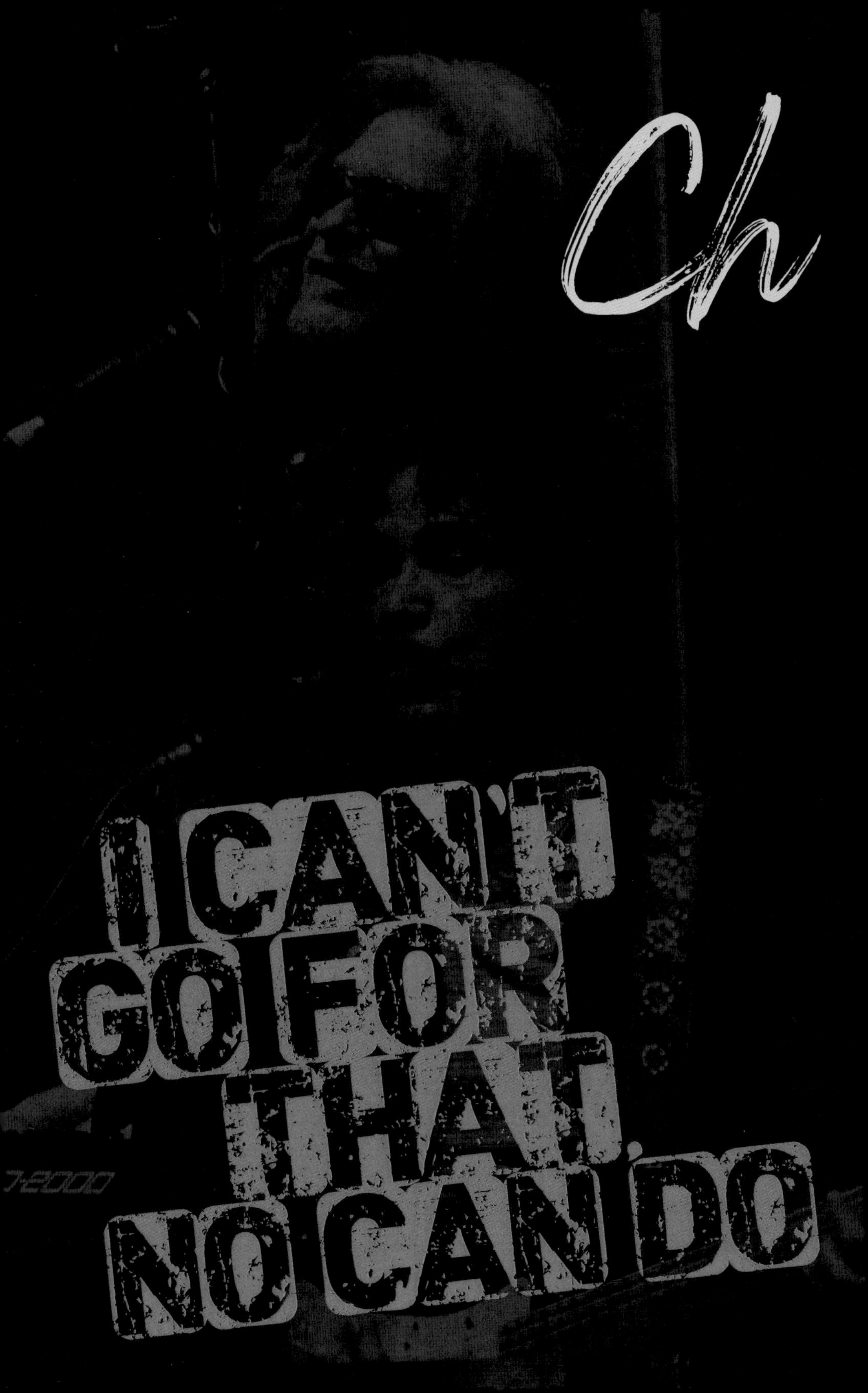
Ch
I CAN'T
GO FOR
THAT
NO CAN DO
7-2000

apter 9

"I Can't Go For That, No Can Do"

The Art of Seeing Shows as a So-Called Mature Adult, and How I Almost Got Into My First Real Rock n Roll Fist Fight... at a Fucking Hall & Oates Concert!

At this point in my life, I've done the mosh, the front row, the crowd surfing, (no stage diving), the sneaking in, the swapping tickets, the printing fake ones, the begging friends, the buying a ticket and canceling the check, the waiting in line, etc. Now I'm older and I'll pay for a fucking seat, thank you very much.

Now I'm the guy with the extra ticket who will sometimes give it to a younger kid who just wants to get in and be a part of the show by any means necessary. I know how he or she feels, and I'm more than happy to pay it forward. And you should too! Five dollars? Sure. One beer? Sure. A kiss on the cheek from your mom or grandma? Definitely. Rock on, kid!

I'm happy to get someone in the building if it's going to blow their mind, make them remember this day forever, and write a book in forty years about all their stupid Rock n Roll adventures.

You are never too young—or too old—to rock.

But these days, I prefer to be just a bit more comfortable, if I can afford to do so. Hey, don't get me wrong—I just literally bought the Lawn Pass to Jiffy Lube Live's 2020 concert season, so I'll be out on the grass with all the pot smokers and beer drinkers for just about every show this season. But as I get older, it gets a little tougher to get up off the grass multiple times per show, so I don't mind paying for a seat now and again.

And if you're in that seat, scream your lungs out. Get up and dance. Sing. Squeal. High-five. Grab your friends and sing along with them. That's what concerts are for. If you don't like that, sit in the lawn and be quiet, or just don't go to a fucking concert at all. Stay at home and watch your favorite band on DVD. No one will bother you. You can pause and take a piss whenever you like. And you don't have to deal with the people who are there to have a good time.

A couple years back, I went to see Hall & Oates at Jiffy Lube. I had never seen them before, and they put out a lot of good music back in the day, so why the hell not. Decent price for tickets, two hours of hit music, and a solid band—I'll take that any time.

They played all their good shit. "Out of Touch," "Private Eyes," "Rich Girl," and my personal favorite from my sixth grade dance, "Maneater." I remember dancing to that song with a couple of the cute girls in my class, and while I'm sure I was doing it all wrong, it's a great memory to a great song.

During each one of those songs and more, me, my friend, and the entire row, would stand up, dance, sing, high-five, hug, and just have the best time we could have.

Well, that didn't seem to go over too well with Mr. Johnny McDoucheBag a few rows behind us. Every time we stood up, other people behind us would stand too. Some would stand to see the show, and others would join us in singing and dancing and having fun. And he was getting more and more pissed off.

First came the yelling.

"Sit down assholes, we're trying to watch a show!"

"What's wrong with you—we can't see the stage."

"There's no way Oates' mustache is still that dark after all these years without some serious hair dye!"

Okay, that last one wasn't real but the other two were—and he wouldn't let up.

We ignored him the best we could, until he decided to come over to our row and make it personal. He started yelling at all the people in the row, calling us names, telling us to "sit the fuck down". And they pretty much ignored him or told him to go back to his seat and dance a little himself, it'll do him good!

And then he got to me.

As you may have surmised by reading this book, I tend to be a bit of smartass from time to time. My mouth has definitely gotten me into trouble over the years, and tonight was going to be no different.

He told me to "fuck off and sit down."

I told him to "make me."

I told him to "relax and enjoy the show."

And then I told him to go back to his wife and entertain her before I went over there and did it for him.

Well, that didn't go over too well with Mr. Johnny McDoucheBag, so he got right in my face.

"I can't go for that, no I, no can do..." was playing in the background, live on stage with one of the best Philadelphia Soul groups of all time.

I got right back in his as well.

"No no no no no no no no can do...." Came the sultry tones of one Mr. Darryl Hall.

Other people started to gather around as well.

"Can't go for that, can't go for that, can't go for that..." Saxophone solo!

At this point, one of two things was going to happen. He was going to make a move. Or he was going to walk away. I didn't back down an inch, but if he wanted to throw a punch, fine, let's do this... in the middle of a fucking Hall & Oates concert. Let's throw the fuck down.

I think he realized the stupidity of what was about to happen, realized I wasn't going anywhere after his Mr. Johnny

McDoucheBag intimidation techniques failed to work, and realized that I had about twenty-thirty people around me, who were also dancing and having fun, and probably would have taken my side if push came to shove.

So, he gave me one final "fuck off" and went back to his seat to entertain his lady.

I'm glad nothing happened. It would have sucked to ruin that show. We both would have been kicked out and I would have missed some classic music.

But I'm also happy it didn't happen, so I didn't have to explain to people for the rest of my life that I never did get into a fight at Rage Against the Machine, Iron Maiden, Guns N Roses, Ozzy, or any of the hundreds of other louder, faster, harder, shows I've been to—but rather at Hall & Oates while they were playing "I Can't Go For That (No Can Do)." Thank god for small favors.

Chapter 9.1

"Believe in the Freedom of Music"

Music has changed quite a bit since I started rocking out. First, came the consolidation that I talked about in an earlier chapter, and then came the digital revolution, which I sort of ignored altogether. We all know the story of Napster, Apple, file sharing, and $.99 downloads, and how some bands will just make music in their den or garage, put in on iTunes, make a fortune, and never perform a live show.

What a joke.

But that's the world we live in, so what's the alternative? Not listen to music at all? I don't fucking think so.

Music is changing, and you have to change along with it.

Buy that download of that one song you heard on that one commercial for Audi, or Miller, or feminine hygiene products.

Why not? Play that song at the gym if it gets you to do one more set or stay on the treadmill a little bit longer.

Go see the reunion tours where each band from the '80s gets thirty minutes to play their three-four hits songs before the next band comes out. In a way, these tours are a bit of a call back to the way they used to be back in the '50s. It's the tours my dad helped organize like the one with Diana Ross and the Supremes, Little Richard, The 5 Royales, etc. We seem to be heading back in that direction, and that's okay.

There are also the MEGA-tours that seem to pop up every summer. Like I said earlier, this year, Guns N Roses is hitting the road again with one of their early line-ups. I looked into tickets, and VIP packages were going for nine-hundred dollars! If that's your thing, go for it.

Then there are the random shows that seem to pop up for no logical reason whatsoever, and you just have to be on the ball and take advantage of those when they come around.

I went to visit a buddy of mine in Green Bay, Wisconsin. He is actually the graphic designer for this book. Super talented dude, and a massive Rock n Roll and metal fan. Craig has a room dedicated in his house to KISS. The KISS man cave is actually where I slept when I went to visit him. I fell asleep to Gene, Paul, Ace, and Peter staring at me every night, while trying to get "Lick it Up", "Deuce", or "I Was Made For Loving You Baby" out of my head. If you're a KISS fan, make your way to Green Bay and knock on his door. He'll be happy to chat with you, I'm sure.

Anyway, Craig and I have spent a lot of time throwing up metal horns at concerts over the years (Def Leppard, Tesla, Cheap Trick, and many others).

But for this trip, I just wanted to go hang with him, meet his lovely family, check out Green Bay, and try something called a cheese curd!

Our plans included a tour of Lambeau Field, which, even though I'm not a Green Bay fan, was absolutely epic, and to go see a Milwaukee Brewers game—because I'm also a big baseball nerd, and want to see all thirty MLB ballparks before I die (as of this book, I'm at fourteen, so I have some work to do!).

But something else caught our attention that three-day weekend. Something we couldn't believe was real.

Something called the Kings of Chaos.

Well, that's kind of a cool name for a band, so let's find out more!

The Kings of Chaos was made up of Sebastian Bach from Skid Row on vocals, Warren DeMartini from Ratt on guitar, Gilby Clarke from GNR on guitar, Matt Sorum from GNR on drums, James LoMenzo from Megadeth on bass, and for this night only, flying in from his New York home, Mr. Ace Fucking Frehley, of KISS fame, on guitar.

Ummmm, excuse me?

These Rock n Roll gods, these metal legends, these music heroes of ours were playing right down the road, in the middle of nowhere, at the Washington County Fairgrounds in West Bend, Wisconsin.

Go ahead, find West Bend, Wisconsin on a map. I'll wait!

After spending probably thousands of dollars to see KISS, Skid Row, Guns N' Roses, Megadeth in my life, now all these guys were going to be playing the County Fair near Green Bay?

And tickets were still available.

We ran to the computer, got online, looked up seats, and bought two tickets.

In the third row.

Holy shit.

We headed south for about ninety minutes and parked in a cow pasture with two really big 'dualie' wheeled trucks on either side of us, and proceeded to slog through the mud to get into the Fair—which was a separate ticket, naturally.

I've been to a few County Fairs in my life and they are just a shit ton of fun. You want country music? Go to Tent #4. Pat

Benatar cover band? Hang a left by the deep fried twinkie stand and go to Tent #7. Want to get hit on by a Washington County financial planner who thought that some guy from the D.C. area was just the cutest thing she's ever seen? Um, where's that Pat Benatar tent again?

But it was just a wonderful opportunity and kudos to the fine folks of Washington County, Wisconsin for putting on such a great experience.

And then came the show.

As you saw in the list chapter, I've seen Skid Row about ten times. And each time, Sebastian and the boys were about the size of a grain of rice. But I never cared. This time, he was life size and right there in front of me. And he was here to have a good time.

I always wondered if the musicians themselves knew how the music experience was changing, for us, the fans. Or did they just want to put on the same show that made them famous back in 1992? To be honest, some are better at this than others. Some don't realize how much it's changed until it's too late, and they've alienated all their fans. Some roll with the changes faster and are able to change their idea of a Rock n Roll show to meet the fans where they are.

That's definitely what happened in Washington County that night.

All the boys were there to have fun, play some hits, do some covers, and rock the five thousand or so fans that came to see them in the cow pasture.

And they did not disappoint.

It seems like every one of my metal heroes from the '80s and '90s grew up as KISS fans. They all had the t-shirts. They all loved the music. And they all dressed up as "Star Child" or "The Cat Man" for Halloween when they were seven years old.

Now they got to play on stage with one of *their* heroes and do some of the songs that he wrote. Epic.

Even from the back row, you could tell these guys were just having a shit ton of fun. Was the music perfect? No. Did someone miss a lyric or two? Probably. Were there too many beers on the side of the stage? Most definitely.

But they were having a blast, and that came through to the appreciative audience who were just happy to see these guys play the songs they love.

And my buddy Craig was a mess too. It was so much fun to watch. Ace probably only played half the show and of that time, did about three-four KISS songs while just playing rhythm guitar to some other songs like "Round and Round" or something from *Deep Purple.*

But Craig was playing air guitar like a motherfucker, singing every lyric, knowing what chord progression was coming next, and still finding time to teach me some KISS history (KISS-tory?) in between the songs.

"That one was recorded in 1975 and first appeared on their *Hotter Than Hell* album."

"Awesome man, rock on!"

We wanted the best and we got the best that night!

We even did the total groupie thing and stuck around by the backstage fence for about an hour after the show just so Craig could see his hero Ace one more time.

Ace never came to the fence, but Sebastian did. He talked to us all for a while, signed autographs, took photos and gave us a few minutes of face time which we will remember forever.

Craig and I sang Skid Row and KISS classics all the way back up to Green Bay before I fell asleep under Gene, Paul, Ace, and Peter's watchful gaze in the KISS Man Cave with a big fucking smile on my face.

So, what am I trying to say? My point with all this is that anything can happen these days when it comes to music. Music isn't dying–it's changing. And you've got to change along with it.

If you live in a small town like Green Bay and need to drive a hundred miles to see some metal heroes, you do it. If you live in a big town and notice that your favorite guitarist's side project is playing a small club, you go see it. If you see that a band you love just put out a new CD, you support it. Buy the CD and rock that shit out in your car, in your home, or at the gym—whenever you can.

Basically, it comes down to this. Stop bitching about how music just isn't the same as when you were a kid. Stop downloading it for free and instead, support your bands. Get up to the front of the stage, stick out your metal horns, and say 'fuck yeah' to that first power chord.

It's the only way to live!

Rock on!

NEW YORK GROOVE
10 AND LIFE
DEUCE
YOUTH GONE WILD
PARADISE CITY
ROUND AND ROUND
DETROIT ROCK CITY
COLD GIN
AND MANY MORE
KINGS OF CHAOS
ROCK'S ULTIMATE SUPERGROUP
ACE FREHLEY
FREHLEY'S COMET • FORMERLY OF KISS
WARREN DeMARTINI
RATT
GILBY CLARKE
FORMERLY OF GUNS N ROSES
SEBASTIAN BACH
ORIGINAL VOICE OF SKID ROW
MATT SORUM
VELVET REVOLVER • GUNS N' ROSES
JAMES LoMENZO
MEGADETH • BLACK LABEL SOCIETY
THIS FRIDAY, JULY 26
WASHINGTON COUNTY FAIR
Join the Movement | kingsofchaosband.com
wcfairpark.com

This was a crazy fun night in the middle of NO-where...!

I can't go for that. No can do

EVENT CODE
EJL0526E
SECTION/AISLE
302
E
SEAT
ADMISSION
COMP
$ 0.00
$
INCL PARKING
LIVE NATION PRESENTS
DARYL HALL & JOHN OATES
WWW.HALLANDOATES.COM
JIFFY LUBE LIVE
* * * * *
THU MAY 26 2016 7PM SHARP
SECTION/AISLE
302
CA 36X
ROW E
SEAT 47
YLA1026
26MAY6
EJL052
CN 517
302
CA609
Trombone Shorty

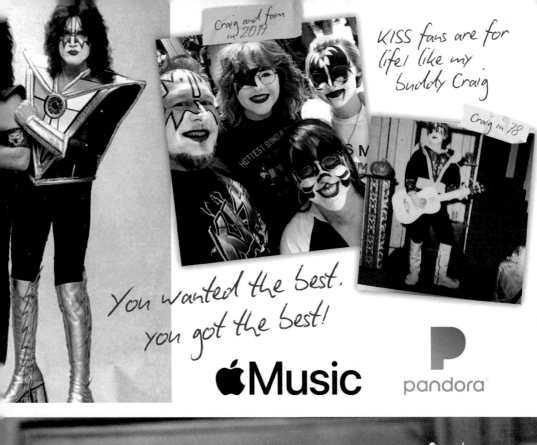

Craig and fam in 2019

KISS fans are for life! like my buddy Craig

Craig in 78

You wanted the best. you got the best!

Music

pandora

Epi
MEGADETH
PANTERA

logue

A Life of Music and Design

An almost-famous music fan once said, "Listen to Tommy with a candle burning and you will see your entire future."

Hell. Yes. That fan was talking about *me*. No, talking TO me.

You read this book, so you know exactly what I'm talking about. Ken is a music fan. I am a music fan. WE. ARE. MUSIC. FANS!

Allow me to set the stage for my frame of reference in all of this. In 1981, I was 13 years old. Vinyl was king, "taping" songs off the radio was normal behavior, MTV was so new it would be three years before my cable provider carried it, and the monthly newsstand rock magazines were my Google.

I was raised in a small town (2,200 people small) in rural Upper Michigan. The nearest movie theater or record store was 50+ miles away, and my exposure to music was television, word of mouth, radio, and those damn magazines. On the rare occasion I was at a record store (or a department store with a record section—I'm looking at you ShopKo) I would take in every section, every album, every poster, everything that had to do with music. The album cover artwork determined what record label was getting my allowance money that month without ever listening to a note.

The day I personally became a music fan was in the fourth grade, and Mrs. Bouche's class had show-and-tell (if you know, you know). My classmate Andy brought in a six-foot tall, four-foot wide poster his older brother bought him of the band KISS. As I stared at the larger-than-life images with makeup and fire, I couldn't get home fast enough to ask my dad to buy me their music. Thankfully he did, and I'm proud to say after 45 years and 20+ concerts, this music fan will ALWAYS be a KISS fan. (Yup, that's me pictured in Chapter 9.)

In the years that followed, it's no coincidence that my path would be creative design. I've spent my career learning and exploring the use of creative design in branding and marketing, and when I found out I could earn a living doing THIS, it was over. I quickly understood why the music was only part of the package. Logos, photography, clothing, tattoos, hair, and so much more are an integral part of the music experience. It's not enough to just listen to music—the experience benefits from sensory and visual support.

To every music fan who held the vinyl sleeve in their hand, read every lyric sheet, sewed a back patch on a jean jacket, or shed a tear when a lyric triggered an emotion, just know we see you. We are you.

I first met Ken back in 2012. A single work-related conference call between two strangers evolved into an over nine-year friendship deeply rooted in, you guessed it, music. While our ages and musical inspirations parallel in many ways, we couldn't have grown up experiencing it more differently. While I was reading and listening to music in Upper Michigan, Ken was out living it in Los Angeles. Not as a musician, but as a FAN. (And yes, he knows I'm totally jealous about it.)

Ken's story is a defining example of WHY music matters. Music can express your emotions without having you show them the way, and takes you places where anything is possible and everything is within reach. Music is an auditory, sensory, and visual art form.

This book was Ken's labor of love. I'm honored to call him friend, and to have played a small role in bringing his book to life. For those who know him, there are many more stories that didn't make it in this edition, but that's what sequels are for. We are ALL music fans, and we all have stories to be shared. Write yours down, tell them to your children, post them online, or write a book of your own.

SHARE your experiences with anyone who will listen because music matters.

Craig

Craig Bower is a life-long music fan with his own KISS room. He's an award-winning creative entrepreneur with 30+ years of design, marketing, and branding experience who is passionate about helping people succeed with the power of visual design. He and his awesome family call Green Bay, Wisconsin home. Through **designthatrocks.com** *he develops marketing and branding strategies that rock, and through* **rubthatrocks.com** *he develops spice blends for damn good BBQ.*

But he'd give it all up to tour with KISS.

Photo Credits

Unless otherwise noted below, photos © 2021 Ken Schwartz.

Chapter 2

Tower Records: http://martinostimemachine.blogspot.com/2017/10/the-legendary-past-and-celluloid-future.html

Pirate Radio Logo: http://www.socalradiohistory.com/kqlz.html

A&M Studios: https://www.discogs.com/label/265722-AM-Studios

Oingo Boingo: https://tvtropes.org/pmwiki/pmwiki.php/Music/OingoBoingo

Chapter 3

Aerosmith & Run DMC Walk This Way Music Video Clips: https://www.imdb.com/title/tt6722960/mediaindex

Ice Cube: https://s.abcnews.com/images/Entertainment/GTY_ice_cube_nwa_2_jt_150814_16x9_992.jpg

Juice Wrld: https://www.dailycardinal.com/staff/andy-fordnme

Chapter 4

Florentine Gardens: https://nightout.com/events/florentine-gardens-hollywood-18-fridays-nightclub-in-los-angeles/tickets

West End Nightclub: https://www.google.com/imgres?imgurl=https%3A%2F%2Flookaside.fbsbx.com%2Flookaside%2Fcrawler%2Fmedia%2F%3Fmedia_id%3D1010989179110090&imgrefurl=https%3A%2F%2Fwww.facebook.com%2Fwestendsantamonica%2F&tbnid=kMAU_R0g-CFeQSM&vet=12ahUKEwibgs61nsXwAhWIBd8KHQsSDSQQMy-gAegQIARBj..i&docid=TuI43r217d8nRM&w=960&h=960&q=The%20

West%20End%20Santa%20Monica%20club&ved=2-ahUKEwibgs61nsXwAhWIBd8KHQsSDSQQMygAegQIARBj

Sony Pictures: https://i.pinimg.com/originals/7f/e1/c8/7fe1c8f17bfc45b2ad53a31e9f378e55.jpg

Legwarmers Band Logo: http://www.jeffersontheater.com/events/detail/the-legwarmers-the-ultimate-80s-tribute-band

Chapter 5
McCabe's Guitar Shop: https://en.wikipedia.org/wiki/McCabe%27s_Guitar_Shop#/media/File:McCabe's_Guitar_Shop,_Santa_Monica.JPG

Possum Dixon: https://pitchfork.com/news/46509-rip-celso-chavez-of-possum-dixon/

Drum Kit: https://www.notsomoderndrummer.com/not-so-modern-drummer/2016/4/28/1976-slingerland-rock-outfit

Chapter 6
'Metal Horns Ken' photograph by Joe Elliot, after Ken handed Joe his personal camera.

Chapter 7
Mosh Pit: https://allabouttherock.co.uk/how-to-survive-a-mosh-pit/

Crowd Surfing: https://www.bucketlist127.com/goal/go-crowd-surfing

Chapter 8
Styx: https://scotterb.wordpress.com/2011/07/01/stalinist-styx/

Lzzy Hale: https://blog.sigmaphoto.com/2018/sigma-art-lenses-for-sony-e-mount-hands-on-report/2000_px-lzzy-hale-in-concert-blue-background/

Ginger Baker: https://www.thetimes.co.uk/article/ginger-baker-obituary-3rmkrwhpg

Music Video Clip from November Rain by Guns N Roses: https://www.kerrang.com/the-news/november-rain-is-the-greatest-music-video-of-all-time-according-to-donald-trump/

Chapter 9

Raph_PH (https://commons.wikimedia.org/wiki/File:Hall_And_Oates_with_Chris_Isaak_-_The_O2_-_Saturday_28th_October_2017_HallOatesO2281017-55_(37601716094).jpg#filelinks), "Hall And Oates with Chris Isaak - The O2 - Saturday 28th October 2017 HallOatesO2281017-55 (37601716094)", https://creativecommons.org/licenses/by/2.0/legalcode

Ken Schwartz 2021 Photograph by Ian Schoenfield.

Hall & Oates: https://simple.wikipedia.org/wiki/Hall_%26_Oates#/media/File:Hall_&_Oates.jpg

KISS: http___com.ft.imagepublish.upp-prod-us.s3.amazonaws.jpeg

Ace Frehley & Sebastian Bach, Young KISS fan and KISS family Photographs by Craig Bower.

Epilogue

Gudellaphoto - stock.adobe.com

About the Author

As the son of legendary record-man, Red Schwartz, Ken desperately wanted to follow in his father's footsteps. He swung for the fences but just couldn't quite get there. But along the way, he worked in music and entertainment, did all kinds of jobs, met a lot of famous people, and gathered a lot of great stories.

Through all that, and even now, his love of music is deep. He keeps up with the music scene, buys way too many albums, and goes to concerts—a lot of concerts. Ken has been to more than 250 shows and seen over 600+ bands. The chance to be with fellow fans and experience Rock n Roll is like nothing else.

For the past 25 years, Ken has worked in marketing, media, and communications for various companies on both coasts and he's always looking for the next great band. He currently lives with his wife, four kids, and grandson, in the Northern Virginia area.

Instagram: @AllTheCoolBands
Twitter: @AllTheCoolBands

Made in the USA
Middletown, DE
11 January 2022

58440216R00111